Always Becoming, Never Arriving

Always Becoming, Never Arriving

Developing an Imagination for Teaching Christianly

DAVID J. MULDER

 CASCADE *Books* • Eugene, Oregon

ALWAYS BECOMING, NEVER ARRIVING
Developing an Imagination for Teaching Christianly

Copyright © 2024 David J. Mulder. All rights reserved. Except for brief quotations in critical publications or reviews, no part of this book may be reproduced in any manner without prior written permission from the publisher. Write: Permissions, Wipf and Stock Publishers, 199 W. 8th Ave., Suite 3, Eugene, OR 97401.

Cascade Books
An Imprint of Wipf and Stock Publishers
199 W. 8th Ave., Suite 3
Eugene, OR 97401

www.wipfandstock.com

PAPERBACK ISBN: 979-8-3852-0506-6
HARDCOVER ISBN: 979-8-3852-0507-3
EBOOK ISBN: 979-8-3852-0508-0

Cataloguing-in-Publication data:

Names: Mulder, David J.

Title: Always becoming, never arriving : developing an imagination for teaching Christianly / David J. Mulder.

Description: Eugene, OR : Cascade Books, 2024 | Includes bibliographical references and index.

Identifiers: ISBN 979-8-3852-0506-6 (paperback) | ISBN 979-8-3852-0507-3 (hardcover) | ISBN 979-8-3852-0508-0 (ebook)

Subjects: LCSH: subject | subject | subject | subject

Classification: CALL NUMBER 2024 (paperback) | CALL NUMBER (ebook)

VERSION NUMBER 12/16/24

Scriptures taken from the Holy Bible, New International Version®, NIV®. Copyright © 1973, 1978, 1984, 2011 by Biblica, Inc.™ Used by permission of Zondervan. All rights reserved worldwide. www.zondervan.com The "NIV" and "New International Version" are trademarks registered in the United States Patent and Trademark Office by Biblica, Inc.™

To Mrs. Ella Aasen,
who started me on the journey of loving learning,

and Dr. John Van Dyk,
who helped me begin to understand teaching Christianly.

Contents

Acknowledgments | ix
Introduction | xi

Chapter 1
Learning to Think like a Teacher: Developing Your "Teacher Imagination" | 1

Chapter 2
The Teaching Profession: Job? Calling? What are We Doing Here Anyway? | 10

Chapter 3
Faith Matters: What is Teaching "Christianly?" | 21

Chapter 4
Joys and Challenges of Teaching Today: History, Reform, and the Future | 31

Chapter 5
Do the Right Thing: Professionalism and Ethics | 40

Chapter 6
Understanding Your Office: Learning and Leading | 50

Chapter 7
Jesus Loves the Little Children: Learner Development | 62

Chapter 8
Jesus Loves ALL the Little Children: Learner Diversity | 74

Chapter 9
Culture and Climate: Creating a Space Where Learning Can Happen | 84

Chapter 10
Knowledge and Understanding: What Do You Need to Know to Be a Teacher? | 93

Chapter 11
Finding the Path: Curriculum Guides the Learning | 104

Chapter 12
Designs for Learning: Planning and Preparation for Effective Instruction | 114

Chapter 13
Getting Inside their Heads: The Most Mystical Part of Teaching | 125

Chapter 14
Effective Instruction: Teaching like Jesus? | 135

Chapter 15
Joy on the Journey: Why We Never "Arrive" at Teaching Christianly | 146

Notes | 159
Bibliography | 171

Acknowledgments

THE IDEA OF THIS book has been rolling around in my head for years, and I'm grateful for the many folks who have had a hand in helping me develop and refine the ideas you'll find within.

My journey into teaching Christianly began with the models I had in my elementary, middle, and high school experiences at Valley Christian Schools in Bellflower and Cerritos, California. Teachers like Ella Aasen, Todd De Jong, Gloria Pelham, Mark Hugen, and John Branderhorst—among many others—gave me examples of what teaching Christianly looked like long before I had any inkling that I would become a teacher myself.

The professors I had in both my undergraduate and graduate studies at Dordt University deeply shaped my understanding of teaching Christianly and helped to form me into the teacher I am today. In particular, I'm grateful to Dennis Vander Plaats who taught several undergraduate methods courses that powerfully impacted my practice, and John Van Dyk and Gloria Goris Stronks who gave me the nudge during my graduate studies to keep experimenting with my practice. Their "permission to play" gave me the confidence to develop my own teaching imagination.

Many excellent teachers have mentored me along the way and helped me develop my imagination for teaching Christianly. My wonderful uncle, Jim Den Ouden, is a longtime Christian educator who has cheered me on every step of the way. Arlan Memmelaar and Marlys Hickox gave me invaluable coaching in those first formative years, and Steve Crull was always an excellent co-conspirator in undertaking daring acts of pedagogy. When I began teaching in higher education, Pat Kornelis, Tim Van Soelen, and Barb Hoekstra were always ready to listen, to support, to nudge me to be better. I worked out a great many of the ideas in this book over the past decade with my dear former colleague, Ed Starkenburg, who thinks deeply

Acknowledgments

about teaching Christianly, and is one of the most encouraging human beings I know. The whole Education Department at Dordt University is incredible, really, and it's a delight for me to serve alongside them today.

It has been a joyful privilege to teach Introduction to Education at Dordt for over ten years, helping these folks who are just beginning to explore the field of teaching to discern their calling, and whether that includes becoming professional educators themselves. A multitude of conversations with future teachers has informed the writing of this book, and I'm so grateful to be able to pull those threads together here.

I have already mentioned John Van Dyk, but I have to say a little more in acknowledgement of his influence in my life. I've used his book *Letters to Lisa* as a text as long as I've taught Introduction to Education. I would like to think of this book as a sort of spiritual successor to that book, as John's extensive work on teaching Christianly has thoroughly saturated my own imagination. I am the professor I am today in no small part due to John's influence in my life, and it's with deep gratitude that I get to follow in his footsteps. Truly, I feel that I'm standing on the shoulders of giants.

Writing this book was a joyful challenge for me, and there are several people who deserve specific thanks for getting it out into the world. I'm grateful for the support of the Kielstra Center at Dordt University that gave me the time and mental space to write this book. The Wednesday Morning Coffee Crew at the Fruited Plain always cheered me on (Justin, Jeremy, Matt, Channon, and Gayle, you folks are the best) and I'm so grateful for you all and the positive influence you've been in my life through the ups and downs of this writing process. My Hallway Conversations podcasting colleagues, Matthew Beimers and Abby De Groot, are always great as a sounding board for ideas I've been playing around with; I'm so glad I get to regularly carve out time with you both to think deeply about our practices as Christian teachers. Thanks to Craig Stiemsma and Ryan Zonnefeld for regularly checking in with me throughout the writing process. And to my wife, Missy, the love of my life, thanks for always giving me a listening ear and an encouraging word in the times when I was running stuck and celebrating with me when I had a breakthrough. I love you more than I can say.

The soundtrack for writing this book was provided by the lovely musicianship of Adam Young, The Oh Hellos, Balmorhea, and Andrew Peterson. I recommend all these artists for your listening pleasure.

Introduction

To the uninitiated, teaching looks straightforward enough. Herd the kids into their desks, open the teacher's manual, have them read from their textbooks, show them a video, assign them a worksheet, and send them off to lunch, right? How hard could it be? It's kind of like babysitting, isn't it? Make sure the kids are safe and busily occupied, and hopefully they learn something too?

Perhaps it's little wonder that many people think this way. Most of us have extensive experience watching teachers at work from the students' side of the desk, and we think we know what teachers do. Really good teachers *do* make it look easy. Perhaps because we've spent so long in classrooms as students, we think we have a pretty good handle on what it takes to teach.

It's not that watching has no value. You can learn a bit about plumbing by watching a plumber at work. You can learn a bit about flying a plane by watching a pilot at the controls. You can learn a bit about how to do surgery by watching a doctor wield her scalpel. But just because you've observed a plumber or pilot or surgeon—or teacher—doing their work doesn't qualify you to *do* the work.

Observing a teacher certainly gives you some insight into the things they do. But here is the problem: if you aren't a teacher, you don't *think like a teacher*. My deep hope for this book is that reading it will give you new and different insight into the work that teachers do, and you might begin to develop a "teacher imagination." That is, I hope it helps you begin to shift in the way you picture what happens in a classroom from thinking like a student to thinking like a teacher.

After reading the title, I'm sure you are not surprised to hear that I think our faith perspective really matters for the work we do as teachers! This book is for Christian teachers in particular, and my second goal for this book is to encourage Christian teachers to carefully examine how their

Introduction

faith impacts every part of their work. This is what I mean by teaching *Christianly*: we recognize that Jesus Christ is King of Kings and Lord of Lords, and we seek to proclaim that truth—in word and in deed—in our classrooms.

This is not a nuts-and-bolts of teaching kind of book, and it's not a philosophical treatise. Rather, this book is meant to help you examine the teaching profession, and ask thoughtful, reflective questions about what it means to teach Christianly. In the process, I hope you'll build up your teacher imagination, and start to look at what happens in classroom with a different understanding and appreciation. Teaching is hard work, but it is *good* work. Developing a teacher imagination for the work of teaching Christianly will help you to both navigate the challenging parts of the profession and celebrate the joyful aspects. In that light, three brief suggestions for how to use this book.

First, please read the short vignettes at the beginning of each chapter. These are imaginary journal entries from a teacher named Taylor who is still relatively new to the profession but has a few years of teaching experience. I've tried to make the teacher gender-neutral so you can put yourself into Taylor's shoes as you read: try and imagine what this teacher is feeling as you read those journal entries.

Second, my hope is that this book lays out the basic landscape of the teaching profession, chapter by chapter. Of course, teaching is too complex and nuanced to get into every aspect of the professional work of teachers in great detail. But I hope that each chapter will stretch your imagination about a slice of the profession. I would encourage you to read just one chapter at a time and spend a little time reflecting on how the ideas from that chapter have expanded your view of what teaching Christianly might look like in practice.

Third, I have included some prompts for reflection with each chapter. I encourage you to *write* responses to these. Writing is thinking! And there is something about documenting your own thinking by writing down your ideas; when you come back to re-read them, it's sometimes surprising what new insights emerge.

Finally, a quick word about the title. I believe in my bones that everyone considering joining the teaching profession is setting out on a journey of "becoming," and that we never fully "arrive" as teachers. There is always more to learn, and places where we can grow! Whether you are a college student who is just discerning whether teaching might be your vocational

Introduction

calling, or a seasoned teacher who might need a little encouragement to recall your passion, I hope this book will help to expand your imagination for teaching Christianly.

Blessings to you as you imagine!

Dr. Dave Mulder
Professor of Education
Dordt University

Chapter 1

Learning to Think like a Teacher
Developing Your "Teacher Imagination"

Taylor's Journal . . .

It is the first day of school for the new school year! I've learned SO MUCH about teaching over these past couple of years. It's not that I wasn't prepared to start my career as a teacher; but as one of my Education professors once put it, the only way too become a 10-year veteran is to go out and teach for 10 years. Watching teachers at work gives you some idea of what teaching is like, but actually doing this teaching thing is a whole different experience. I keep learning new things on a weekly basis . . . good thing I love to learn!

    The biggest lesson I think I've learned is how to *think* like a teacher. It's funny . . . when I was first considering becoming a teacher, I sort of figured it would be easy. Get the kids to sit down and be quiet, read the story aloud, talk them through the plan for the activity for today, turn them loose, and watch the learning happen! And I guess it's not that I was completely wrong to think that way. Sometimes—when things are going "just so" and everything is just clicking—that is the way it feels. But some days, teaching is just plain *hard work. That was something I never realized when I was watching my own teachers at work.*

But here we go, launching into the adventure of a new year! I know there will be ups and downs, but I also know that I will keep getting better as I keep on experimenting with what I'm doing. I'm here to teach, and I'm here to learn!

You've Had a Long Internship . . .

Teaching is a fascinating profession! The work teachers do is intensely personal while simultaneously being extremely public. Teaching is deeply personal; teachers draw from their personal stores of knowledge, techniques, and lived experiences in practically every part of the work they do, from planning lessons, to connecting with students, to communicating with parents. At the same time, the very nature of what teachers do is public: we constantly conduct our craft in front of people, not least of these being our students.

I've often joked that students have a long internship into the work that teachers do, and it's amazing that more people don't want to become teachers after observing teachers for so many years! From ages 5–18, most children and young people spend a significant part of their waking hours engaged in educational activities, and almost all of this is led by a teacher. While the specific work teachers do may vary at different grade levels, and in different content areas, and in different kinds of schools, the reality is that students have a lot of experience in watching teachers at work. Perhaps it's no wonder then that people think they know what teachers do?

This long internship certainly does give students insight into some aspects of the teacher's work. How could it not? Formal education is almost entirely guided and directed by teachers! But students typically only see the public side of their teacher's work. The personal side of a teacher's work is often hidden from students or conducted in such a way that students are not aware of the work. This makes sense because students, naturally, think like students, not teachers.

Shifting From Thinking Like a Student to Thinking Like a Teacher

When situated in the student's seat, we see the classroom through a student's eyes. We see the teacher at work in a particular way, doing things for us—or sometimes *to* us—that causes us to respond. We know our experience as students, and we observe the teacher's experience as outsiders, usually not slowing down to think about what happens in the classroom from the teacher's perspective, since that is not our perspective, as students. What is actually taking place in the classroom? Our role in a classroom interaction shapes the way we think about what's going on. Let's explore a common classroom scenario from each of these perspectives.

First, let's consider the student's experience. The teacher says, "Please take out your notebooks," and as a student we decide in a flash: comply, or resist? Most students comply; we recognize that the teacher has an authority because of the role they play in the classroom environment, and we do what is asked of us. A few students might sluggishly move as directed, seeming passive-aggressive in their delay. And one or two might not follow the teacher's direction at all . . . whether defiantly or absentmindedly. But all the students have some sense of what is being asked of them: students in the scenario almost certainly know that they are about to do some kind of writing, because that's what teachers expect students to do. And, because of their role in contrast with the teachers' role, students might not even question the action of opening a notebook in class.

But as we shift into the role of the teacher, the simple request that students take out their notebooks suddenly becomes much more complex if we have eyes to see. Sitting in the teacher's seat, we could begin to ask lots of questions about this seemingly-simple request. *Why* are we asking students to take out their notebooks? What are students going to be writing? Are they noting things they observe and notice? Are they copying text off a screen or transcribing words the teacher speaks? Are they capturing their own thinking, or documenting the ideas of others? Are they recording their own questions and wonderings about the world? Can all students in the class write with the same dexterity and fluency? If not, should we make accommodations for the difference in ability? Does writing in a notebook look different for students in first grade and fifth grade and tenth grade? Does writing in a notebook look different for students in history class than it does in math class? Will this writing be graded? And if so, how will the writing be evaluated? How does this particular writing fit in with the rest of learning in this classroom—if it is an essential part of students achieving the course goals, are there alternative routes that could help them hit the learning targets? And should students be using notebooks at all? What does the notebook as a tool for learning do to classroom community? Does it enhance the learning environment, or limit possibilities?

When we are situated in the teacher's seat in the classroom, things may start to appear quite differently than they did from the student's seat. Something as straightforward as asking students to take out a notebook can be much more nuanced and multilayered than the simple task students see! Behind that simple request is a heap of teacher-thinking: knowledge of student development and diversity, various teaching methods and assessment strategies, approaches to help students engage the content being taught, the broader structure of the curriculum for the course, techniques for motivation and classroom management, the culture and climate of the classroom environment, and more. Teachers have a whole private universe behind even the simplest of moves in the classroom, one that goes almost entirely unobserved by students.

The Work of Imagination

What do teachers need most to be effective in the classroom? There are many ways to answer that question. Knowledge of content is certainly important. So too is knowledge about students—how they learn, how they grow and develop, and how individual differences impact learning are all important parts of effective teaching. And knowledge about the work of teaching that is obviously necessary; knowing how to plan lessons, how to use different teaching strategies, and how to assess learning are all essentially important. Knowledge about human behavior, and how to effectively manage students to create a productive classroom atmosphere is clearly valuable. Understanding of professional requirements, ethical behavior, communication strategies, and technical abilities are all foundational requirements to be an effective educator in today's school context. There are many things teachers need to be effective in the classroom!

It might surprise you then, that I will suggest that while *all* of these are important—and necessary!—there is something else I believe teachers need most to be truly effective in the classroom. Teachers need *imagination*.

We often limit imagination to something that is part of childhood, something we grow out of as we become more mature and sophisticated.

Learning to Think like a Teacher

We might associate imagination with "make-believe," our just-pretend games from when we were young. This is a tragedy! Imagination is one of the most important aspects of what makes us human; our capacity to see beyond *what is* to be conceiving *what could be* is an amazing part of how God has created us to be. Imagination is central to who we are, not just as children, but also as adults. Developing our capabilities to take realistic stock of current realities while *also* imagining other possibilities is one of the most important things teachers can do to become truly effective.

How can we do this "imagination work?" I am not sure there is a tidy answer to that question. The work of imagination probably appears quite differently in different content areas, and at different grade levels, and at different points in a teacher's career. Indeed, this is what I've been playing around with throughout my teaching practice so far.

Did you notice how I phrased that last sentence? I want to specifically call your attention to something a moment. In my depiction of the work of imagination for teachers, I used the words "play" and "practice." I chose these two words intentionally, because I believe they are central to developing a teacher imagination.

We should think of the work of imagination as *play* because imagination *is* playful. The fact that we might tend to think of imagination as the pretending that children do as they play illustrates this. But play is important for adults just as it is for children. And play is not the opposite of work, despite a widely held cultural belief that work is hard, and play is leisurely. Work can be both demanding and playful at the same time. The work of teaching is often playful, or at least can be. When we approach teaching with a playful, imaginative spirit it will likely be joyful, fulfilling, inspiring work—something we *get to* do, rather than *have to* do.

We should also think of the work of imagination as *practice* because we can get better at imagining as we invest more time into it. I think that many people equate "imagination" with "creativity." While these two concepts are certainly related, I do not think they are the same thing. Imagination is the capacity to conceive of what could be. Creativity is generativity: when we are creating, we are making. Some creating is imaginative, but it's also possible to slavishly make things (create things) without any imagination. Real imaginative work will almost certainly be creative, whether we produce tangible artifacts or not. The work of imagination is about creating new ideas, new ways of thinking, new approaches, new solutions. And in the same way that practicing kicking a football or practicing scales on your cello makes those skills more fluid, natural, and automatic, practicing imagination has the same kinds of effects on our work.

Teachers certainly need knowledge and skills to be effective, but knowledge and skills are not enough. Teachers who want to grow into the most effective teachers they can become must embrace playfulness and practice as key aspects of their growth. Being able to imagine beyond *what is* into *what could be* is the most important part of learning to truly think like a teacher—to develop a teacher imagination.

The Role of Technique

That last bit might sound like I'm minimizing the importance of technique. I want to say more on that for a moment. Mastering specific techniques certainly *is* important to be effective as a teacher. What do I mean by techniques? Maybe it helps to define "techniques" for teaching as the strategies, and approaches, and protocols, and habits of mind we might use to help students learn. These techniques are important and valuable; having a variety of tools in your toolbox means you are better equipped to respond to what students need in the moment.

There are so many different techniques that teachers use, it can be hard to start making a list, but perhaps a few examples would be helpful to illustrate what I mean. Think about your own experiences in classrooms. Were there particular routines your teachers used for how you would turn in your schoolwork, or how they would take attendance, or how you would use technology in the classroom? Were there norms for classroom interactions (like "raise your hand if you have something to share") or for when you could leave the classroom? Were there go-to teaching approaches that your teachers implemented, like using a slide deck as visual aids for a lecture, or particular protocols to guide discussions? Were there patterns for how your teachers would find out what you had learned, like unit tests, or pop quizzes, or free-writes, or checklists for skills? Were there specific strategies your teachers used for making groups, or calling the class to attention, or managing materials in the classroom? All of these are different kinds of techniques that teachers use, and they are each valuable for helping teachers manage the workload of interacting with groups of students—and ensuring that they will learn.

So, I want to be clear that I am *not* minimizing the importance of technique. Clearly there are strategies, and approaches, and protocols that will help you to be effective in your teaching! And it is important to be mindful of the techniques you decide to employ in your teaching. What I am arguing here is that technique alone is not *enough*.

Teaching is much, much more than just the techniques we use for preparing lessons, or managing the classroom, or assessing students' learning. In his book *The Courage to Teach*, Parker J. Palmer shares this wisdom: "Technique is what teachers use until the real teacher arrives."[1] This is very much how I think of the work of teaching as well! Technique will get you so far, but it won't turn you into a teacher. Focusing only on technique reduces the rich, complex work of teaching, turning the teacher into a mere technician. But when the *real* teacher shows up? That's where the magic begins to happen!

When the Teacher Shows Up . . .

Truly *becoming* a teacher, and not just relying on techniques that teachers use is what this book is really about. My idea of developing an imagination for teaching is central to this. To become a teacher—the *real* teacher, not just a technician—you must be able to imagine the work we get to do as something bigger, something with more importance and lasting impact.

Palmer encourages educators to consider *who we are*, and how our identity and integrity shape what we do as teachers.[2] What is your identity? You might say it's all the things that make you uniquely *you*. And integrity? While we might commonly use the word integrity to mean something along the lines of "doing the right thing," Palmer uses it more in the sense of wholeness—being integral, being integrated, having integrity. In this view, *being* a teacher means knowing who you are (your identity) and knowing how it all holds together as the real you (the integral nature of being a whole person).

An analogy here might be helpful. Imagine that you are an actor. In playing a role, you step onstage, the lights come up and you embody a character. But at the end of the show, the curtain comes down, and you head backstage and become "yourself" again. You are acting, using techniques you have learned and practiced as you interact with the rest of the cast and to engage with the audience. But *you* are not the person you are portraying; you are a different person backstage than you are onstage.

Becoming a teacher can be similar. It is certainly possible for people to act like teachers, to use teaching techniques that will help them to manage classroom life fairly well. But this is really acting, not truly teaching. If you are a different person "backstage" than you are "onstage," are you really the teacher? Palmer calls this living a divided life,³ and he explains that this will not result in effective teaching in the long term. I will go even further and suggest that merely acting like a teacher misses the mark for the real work that teachers get to do. And what is this real work? Teaching is more than just conveying information; a real education is about formation.⁴ True teachers have a hand in shaping who their students are, and how they will be in the world. This is an awesome responsibility, for sure!

Developing a teaching imagination means understanding that the role you are playing in the classroom is *you*—your very own self!—with everything that comes from your identity and integrity. Technique can get you so far . . . but when the teacher shows up, the potential for real impact in students' lives, for the real work of formation and even for transformation too begin becomes possible.

Does Faith Really Matter?—Developing A *Christian* Imagination for Teaching

This work of formation might sound a bit intimidating, and truly it is a big deal! We should approach the work of real teaching with appropriate humility. You might be thinking at this point, "I know myself . . . with all my shortcomings . . . and I am not up for the challenge of becoming a 'real' teacher." I understand this impulse all too well; it is easy for us to see our faults and failures, and perhaps think that they exclude us from becoming truly effective teachers.

This is where the work of imagination comes in, and this importance of developing a *Christian* imagination for teaching. Think again about the nature of our identity and integrity as we discussed earlier. Who are you? Deep down, at your core, who are you?

I'll use myself as an example. I can describe myself by my personal characteristics: I am tall and gangly, I am positive and enthusiastic, I am worried about what other people think of me. I can describe myself by naming my hobbies and activities: I play the guitar and the ukulele, I love to ride my bike, I enjoy trying new foods. I can describe myself by my likes and dislikes: I love cookie dough ice cream, fall is my favorite season of the year, I prefer nineties alternative rock to country music. Each of these descriptors tells you something about who I am. But I can also describe myself by naming important relationships in my life: I am a husband, a father, a son, a brother, a friend, a mentor, a professor, a camp counselor, a church member, a worship leader. Each of these relationships also tells you something about me.

In the same way that I can describe other parts of my life, as a Christian, I can describe myself both by my characteristics and by relationships as well. Who am I? I am created in the image of God. I am a sinner. I am saved by grace through faith in Jesus Christ. I am growing in understanding what it means to follow Jesus. I am empowered by the Holy Spirit. I have spiritual gifts that I can use for the good of others and to God's glory. I am invited to participate in God's ongoing work in this world—what an amazing thought!

When it comes to truly becoming a teacher, our identity matters. Recognizing who you are—who you *really* are in Christ and the full implications of this identity—will impact the way you view your work. As we explore a teaching imagination, we'll continually come back to this idea that our identity in Christ really matters. What is Jesus really calling us to do? How is he calling us to be? Developing a Christian imagination for teaching will illuminate the joys and challenges of the work of teaching in an entirely new way.

Questions for Reflection after Reading

1. Do Parker Palmer's ideas about identity and integrity resonate with you and your vision of the teaching profession? Why or why not?
2. What is a new idea that helped expand your imagination?
3. What challenged your thinking, or what question would you like answered?

Chapter 2

The Teaching Profession
Job? Calling? What are We Doing Here Anyway?

Taylor's Journal . . .

Ooof . . . today was a whiplash kind of day, where I feel like my head was just snapped back and forth. I intervened to stop a scuffle in the hallway just as things were starting to get physical between two boys who were shoving each other. Right after that, I had what might have been the best science lesson I've taught this year. (Praise God! I wasn't sure if the students would go for my crazy idea for determining which brand of paper towels was "best.") But later in the day, I caught Travis lying to my face, and he absolutely refused to back down. I'm dreading calling home about this one, because I remember how defensive his mom was last time I talked to her. Ugh. But then, at the end of the day, Grace and Kassidy offered to tidy up our classroom, just because—and it sure needed it. They are so sweet, and it was just what I needed at the end of a day full of . . . everything.

    I keep reading things about how society doesn't seem to value the work teachers do, and I sure have moments where I feel that is true. And there are plenty of times when I think *my own standards for myself are too high, but I can't help it: I just want to do well for my students, and I put a lot of pressure on myself to do it. "It's for the children," right? This job sometimes feels like more than just a job!*

Teaching: It Isn't Easy!

I love to teach. Since graduating from college, my whole working life has been as a professional educator, and I truly have found it to be the most joyful profession I can imagine. The delight of coming alongside students, unveiling some aspect of creation to them, helping them come to comprehend a new concept, seeing their eyes light up with the spark of understanding . . . I could not ask for a more wonderful way to make a living! The delightful challenge of creating a classroom atmosphere where all students belong and find purpose in learning is demanding, but also so fulfilling. I always feel a sense of pleasure when my lesson design prompts students to wonder and ask their own questions, and the gratification they feel when they have discovered answers for themselves is always inspiring. The wonder of nudging students to reflect on their place in this world is never lost on me. There are so many blessings in this work that I never would have known had I not become a teacher.

As much as I believe teaching is an incredible profession and one I have found to be the most joyful, inspirational work I can imagine, it is *not easy*. Teaching is incredibly complex and requires a wide range of knowledge and skills to do even passably well. Anyone who thinks that teaching is "easy" should step up and volunteer to serve as a substitute teacher for a few days. First-hand experiences might open their eyes to the demands of the profession. Imagine someone with no training in classroom management trying to organize learning in a classroom of 25 kindergartners, where they regularly move on to a new activity every 15–30 minutes. Imagine someone with no training in human development teaching 150 middle school math students throughout the day with diverse levels of cognitive, physical, social, and emotional development. Imagine someone with no training in instructional techniques trying to hook grade 12 students on Shakespeare in their British literature class, when they are so affected by "senioritis" that their motivation to learn is nearly non-existent. Teaching is not "easy" by any stretch of the imagination.

For all the joy I find as a professional educator, it is also the most agonizingly difficult thing I've ever done. Teaching is dangerous work, after all. The danger of teaching is the personal-public nature of work. Much of the work we do as teachers is very public, and we cannot avoid this. The reality is that every time I step into the classroom, I am putting my very self on display in the work I am doing, and this makes me subject to the slings and arrows of embarrassment, criticism, and judgment. The attacks on my identity can come from many places: from my students, from their families, from society, and even from myself.

Those Challenging Students...

Students are wonderful human beings, and yet what horribly alien creatures they can be! Students as individuals are almost always good-natured and kind in one-on-one interactions, which makes working with students very enjoyable. And most students will at the very least be compliant with teachers' expectations, if not eager to join in, within a group setting. The chemistry among the members of a group, however, can cause unpredictable results with even the most enjoyable individuals. Most teachers will agree that within a classroom full of students it is likely that there will be at least one or two "challenging" students. But sometimes a class might have many students who are "challenging" when grouped together. (I can remember some years when I felt like I didn't have enough corners in my classroom to spread out the students who needed a little more distance from each other.) Students are not immune to the effects of sin in the world, and their behavior can illustrate this clearly. From nasty comments directed at either the teacher or at fellow students, to anti-social behavior and bullying, to apathy or even subversion of the classroom climate, students can be demoralizing and difficult. Even when their behavior is developmentally appropriate, it is not always socially appropriate. All of this can take a real toll on teachers who care deeply for their students.

Those Difficult Parents...

As challenging as students can be, working with their families can be even more demanding. Some parents' expectations place an almost unbearable weight on the shoulders of their child's teachers. Some parents expect teachers to be examples of virtue in every way, even to the point of being unrealistically perfect. And while teachers obviously must be ethical, and should be models of character for their students, they are also human; no one can be perfect on a daily basis! Beyond these expectations for teacher behavior, parents also want their children to learn, and have high expectations of teachers' work with their children. Many parents want and expect personalized learning experiences tailored to their child's unique strengths and weaknesses. While teachers can and should plan instruction that meets the needs of every student in their charge, writing individualized lesson plans for each child is not realistic—or even possible—with a whole class of students. Parents also expect, and even demand, clear ongoing communication about what is happening at school, but might be far less communicative with teachers about what is happening at home. While the ideal educational situation is a partnership between home and school, this is unfortunately not always the case.

Societal Pressures

Widening the circle a bit, we should also consider the broader societal context of education. Over the past few decades, increasing demands on the whole educational enterprise have added to the challenges of teaching today. Teachers are expected to play an increasingly broad role in society in ways that go far beyond the primary work of ensuring that students learn. Teachers are expected to be the front line for caring for students' physical and mental health, ensuring they are getting adequate nutrition, keeping them safe from abuse as mandatory reporters, promoting appropriate socialization, and even keeping them physically safe from potential school intruders. In terms of curriculum, decisions made by politicians and policy-makers directly impact not only what teachers teach, but also how they must (or must not) talk about certain issues.

While society on the whole holds up teaching as a noble profession, because of the work teachers do to prepare and equip the next generation, teachers are also often demonized as having the wrong motives for wanting to work with children, including a desire to indoctrinate them according to particular political, social, or religious agendas. And, of course, the real work of teaching—ensuring student learning—is expected to be measured by high-stakes standardized tests, with the outcomes scrutinized and dissected by non-educators who make sweeping judgments about the teaching profession based on these results.

We also should keep in mind the relatively low pay teachers earn. I suspect you might already know that teachers don't make a lot of money considering the incredible importance of what we do? Compared to other professions that require a similar amount of education, teacher pay is relatively low. There certainly are calls from many quarters to increase teachers' pay, but this is the current reality. The lag of teacher compensation behind that of other professions is one very tangible way to picture the societal view of the teaching profession. If society placed a higher value on the work teachers do, perhaps teacher pay would increase.

All these competing pressures are challenging for teachers who got into the profession to make a difference in the lives of their students and find themselves in a web of competing societal demands.

Personal Pressures

Personal pressures are perhaps the most insidious challenge for teachers. The work of teaching is demanding; it is not uncommon for teachers to work ten-hour days to keep up with the planning and assessment tasks. These hours are often invisible work, as they happen outside the view of students and parents. Yet the work must get done, and so teachers sometimes sacrifice personal time for the good of their students' learning. Many teachers feel the weight of expectations placed on through the work, but they also put more weight and more expectations on themselves, dissecting their lessons that didn't go as well as they wished to try and discern where things went sideways and how to keep that from happening again. Many teachers feel a heavy burden for their students, often for things that they cannot change. And yet, teachers critique themselves harshly, forgetting the 97 great things they were able to achieve in a day working with students, and remembering every part of the three missteps they made along the way in vivid detail. The old adage that we are our own worst critics seems to be almost universally true for teachers.

Is Teaching Just a Job?

Thinking through all these challenges might cause despair; this job is just too hard for people to want to do it! Thinking about the difficulties for teachers that arise from students, families, society, and even our own self-criticism, why would anyone want to join the teaching profession?

As much as I love my work as a teacher, I am not naïve to the challenges. Teaching is very demanding work under the best of circumstances, and the demands do not seem to be decreasing. And yet, even in the face of challenges, I am optimistic about the work teachers do, and the difference they make. Teaching is more than just a job. I believe teaching is a calling.

I want to be a little cautious using this language of calling. I think there are many situations when "calling" can be used to mean "sacrifice." For example, there are some people who would justify teachers' relatively low pay by using the language of calling. People might say things to teachers like, "It's okay that you don't make very much money, because teaching is your *calling*," or "People don't become teachers for the *income* . . . they do it for the *outcome*." Statements like these miss an important point: teaching *is* a job, and one that requires special training and a very specific set of skills. Teachers should be well-supported, well-equipped, and well-compensated for the essential work they are doing! Expecting teachers to be willing to sacrifice themselves to do their work is problematic at best and exploitative at worst.

We should think of teaching as a job, and a very demanding one at that! But is teaching *more* than just a job? I think that it is. Teachers that view their work as *just* a job will burn out quickly. As I noted before, I think that we should think of teaching as a calling. This might sound as though I'm trying to have it both ways—that "teaching is just a job" and that "teaching is a high calling." This certainly is a nuanced view! The work is hard, but also deeply fulfilling. The students we teach may be challenging, but it's also an incredible blessing to have a hand in shaping the way young people understand the world and their place in it. The support teachers receive from families may be varied, but overall, every parent wants their kids to have an excellent education. Society at large might seem to denigrate teachers, but teachers also play a crucial role in influencing the future of society. Teachers may put tons of pressure on themselves to perform at high levels, but they also have amazing opportunities to continue growing, developing, and making a difference in the lives of a multitude of people.

There is a complexity to thinking about teaching in this both-and way. A more fully formed view of calling might be needed to understand how to view teaching as more than a job.

How Christians Get "Calling" Wrong

Many Christians like to talk about calling, in the sense that they are "answering God's calling" in their lives. Perhaps this is no wonder; when we read the stories in Scripture, we can see countless examples of people that God called to specific roles. The stories of Patriarch Abraham, and Law-Giver Moses, and Prophet-Judge Samuel, and King David, and dozens of others throughout the Old Testament give evidence of this. In the New Testament, the Apostle Paul's dramatic conversion story of flipping from persecutor to missionary is a compelling depiction of the impact of responding to God's call. And certainly, the stories of Jesus's calling of his disciples by saying, "Follow me!" gives us a sense that there is something specific about God's calling.

There is one story of calling in the Bible that has always captured my imagination. The book of Jeremiah opens with his recounting of how God called him to serve as a prophet. Jeremiah hears God's voice:

> "Before I formed you in the womb I knew you;
> Before you were born I set you apart.
> I appointed you as a prophet to the nations."[5]

Jeremiah's response to God's calling? He says:

> "Ah, sovereign Lord,' I said, 'I do not know how to speak. I am only a child."[6]

But the Lord isn't having any of that! God's response to Jeremiah is clear, and a little terrifying:

> The Lord said to me, "Do not say, 'I am too young.' You must go to everyone I send you to and say whatever I command you. Do not be afraid of them, for I am with you and will rescue you," declares the Lord. Then the Lord reached out his hand and touched my mouth and said to me, "I have put my words in your mouth. See, today I appoint you over nations and kingdoms to uproot and tear down, to destroy and overthrow, to build and to plant."[7]

God clearly has specific plans for Jeremiah—so specific that he calls him by name, and describes exactly what his intentions are, and the way he is equipping Jeremiah for the task God has prepared for him.

Speaking only for myself, I am jealous of Jeremiah. I'm not jealous of the work God called him to; if you read the rest of the book of Jeremiah you will find that he had an incredibly difficult life, and though God was with him in every part of his struggles . . . Jeremiah definitely had struggles. No, I'm jealous of the clarity of the calling Jeremiah received.

There have been seasons of my life when I have been trying to discern what I should do when I felt that God's calling was opaque and unclear. I know I am not alone in this; many fellow believers can tell tales of seeking to discern God's calling in their lives. I wish that I too could hear God's voice giving me specific direction about his will for my life. Maybe the Lord could give me a burning bush moment like Moses? Or call out to me at night like Samuel? Or knock me off my feet on the road to Damascus like Paul?

At the risk of sounding sacrilegious, I think that reading the Bible has set me up to expect that people always receive a calling from God in a spectacular way. In truth, the problem is not the Bible; the problem is *me*. In my sinful human nature, I want to be "special," like those biblical heroes who receive specific calling from the Lord with clear directives on what they are supposed to do. But here is where I think many Christians—myself included—get "calling" wrong.

I have good news for you! Are you ready for it? Here's the thing: you *have* received a specific calling from the Lord, and so have I. The whole of Scripture points to your calling, to what you are supposed to do: if you are a Christian, your calling is to *follow Jesus*. Jesus specifically says, "Whoever wants to be my disciple must deny themselves and take up their cross and follow me."[8] This might not feel like the kind of dramatic calling of hearing God's voice, but don't miss what is happening here: Jesus himself is giving you a specific task to do! This is a spectacular story of receiving your calling, similarly wondrous to the ones people in the stories of Scripture have received. Rather than a burning bush, the Lord ensured that a book would end up in your hands that gives you a special revelation from God himself: if you are a Christian, you are *called* to follow Jesus.

A Biblical View of Vocation

At several point in my life, I have grappled with making a choice, feeling like I desperately wanted to follow God's will and struggling to see what he was truly calling me into. Often these weighty moments were related to my job: should I move across the country to take a teaching job in a new place? Should I pursue a different position in my school? Should I take on this new responsibility? God, give me clarity in my vocation!

Vocation is a word that we often use as a synonym for "work," or "career," or "occupation." But there is more to the word "vocation" than might first meet the eye. The root of this word comes from the Latin word *vocare*, which shows up as the root several other English words, including vocal, voice, and vociferous. What does this word mean? It means summoning, inviting, bidding, calling. Calling? Ah, here we are: the word "vocation" means "calling!" Your vocation is, in fact, much more than just a job . . . your vocation is your *calling*. As Steven Garber puts it,

> The word vocation is a rich one, having to address the wholeness of life, the range of relationships and responsibilities. Work, yes, but also families, and neighbors, and citizenship . . . all of this and more is seen as vocation, that to which I am called as a human being, living my life before the face of God. [*Vocation*] is never the same word as *occupation*, just as *calling* is never the same word as *career*. Sometimes, by grace, the words and the realities they represent do overlap, even significantly; sometimes, in the incompleteness of life in a fallen world, there is not much overlap at all.[9]

Here is a biblical insight into what it is you are called to do: if you are a Christian, your vocation is to *follow Jesus*. Jesus's call to his would-be disciples is, "Follow me." He calls you to follow.

I hope this is a word of comfort and encouragement to you, particularly in times when you are trying to discern God's will for your life. Perhaps it gives you—like me—a chance to lower what can feel like very high stakes a bit. Since coming to reimagine my "vocation" this way, I am freed to ask the question, "Can I faithfully follow Jesus if I am heading down this path?" And if the answer is yes, I think this is an indication that I am following God's will for my life, responding to his calling, living into my vocation.

Maybe this feels a little too loose for you though, not specific enough? There certainly are individuals in the Bible who are given a very specific and narrow calling, like Jeremiah. ("Before you were born, I set you apart . . . ") And I too want that kind of specific calling in my life, honestly. I wish God would say, "Before you were born, I set you apart to be a Christian teacher!" This does not seem to be the way the Lord works in most situations, however. But this is not something we need to lament! The broader sense of calling—of vocation—as *faithfully following Jesus* is in fact a blessing for us. It bids us to do the joyful work of discerning our identity, and understanding how God has uniquely gifted us, and how we can see these gifts as part of his equipping of us for many possible ways to live out our vocation. Garber encourages us in this work of discernment by inviting us to ask the question, "Knowing what I know about the way the world is, what am I going to do?"[10]

This broader sense of calling is an invitation, an invitation to participate in the ongoing work of restoration God is doing in this broken-but-beautiful world. Christians, as members of Christ's body, are invited to work towards the renewal of all things. Fredrick Buechner's often-quoted thought on the meaning of vocation gets at this invitation: "The place God calls you to is the place where your deep gladness and the world's deep hunger meet."[11] What a thought, and what an invitation!

This is the discerning work we get to do then: let's notice how God has created us: what gifts, and talents, and strengths, and passions do you have—and how these bring you joy and delight? Let's also have a look around at the world: what broken places, hungry places can you see? And then the key: how can you faithfully follow Jesus, using what God has given you to joyfully work towards addressing those broken places?

Called to Teach

The question raised throughout this chapter is, "What is this teaching thing about? Is it a job? A calling? What are we doing here anyway?" Teaching certainly is a job. Teachers are professionals with specific knowledge and skills, and are compensated for the work that they do. But is teaching more than *just* a job? For Christian teachers, I think that the answer must be a heart-felt, "Yes!"

Is teaching a calling? My answer is yes; we are called to teach. I suspect that you did not hear the Lord's voice audibly from the clouds, though that is certainly possible. More likely, you've found yourself reading this book after some thoughtful discernment. Perhaps you've noticed how much you love spending time with kids. Maybe there is a particular subject that you simply adore. Maybe your life was profoundly impacted by a teacher, and you have realized that you want to have that kind of impact in the lives of others. Maybe someone else has named your gifts and suggested that you would be a great teacher. God uses many ways to help us become aware of how he equips us for responding too Jesus's call: "Follow me!"

If we are open to the broad view of calling as faithfully following Jesus wherever he might lead us, teaching is definitely a calling for Christian teachers. Teaching is a way for you to seriously seek to live out your faith.

Teaching is a way to use your gifts to educate young people and have a hand their formation as they grow and develop. Teaching is an opportunity to declare "Jesus is Lord!" through your daily work. You are called to teach!

Questions for Reflection after Reading

1. Does the idea of "calling" in this chapter help you better understand the work of teaching? Why or why not?
2. What is a new idea that helped expand your imagination?
3. What challenged your thinking, or what question would you like answered?

Chapter 3

Faith Matters

What is Teaching "Christianly?"

Taylor's Journal . . .

I love my students. I love my students. I love my students. On days like this one, I have to remind myself. It was a rough one with Charlie, and Drew, and Micah today—they were just running wild, and it felt like all I was doing was managing behavior today. And if Ashley and Kaida could stop be so catty with each other and get along for just one day, boy would my life be easier. Their drama seems to get the rest of the girls all riled up every time!

It's an easy thing to say "I believe that each of my students is created in God's image"—and I DO believe that!—but it's harder to follow through with that belief when they are so awful to each other, and to me too. I know Jesus said to love our neighbors as we love ourselves, but on a day like today I kinda want to ask him, "Jesus, do my students count as my neighbors too?" Because while I definitely love them, I don't always like them Or, at least, I don't like their behavior. I guess today I'm just wondering how much my faith *actually has to do with what happens in my classroom. Ugh . . . saying that has me feeling like a part-time Christian . . .*

The Three Loves All Teachers Need

So far in this book we've been talking about the occupation of teaching broadly, and the joys and challenges that the work of teaching bring for those who become professional educators. We've explored identity and integrity, and how technique only gets you so far until the real teacher shows up. We've considered a biblically-informed view of calling in both the broad strokes as well as the specifics of what it means to be called to teach. Now let's shift our attention a bit to thinking about love, and how love influences our work as teachers. I believe that to be truly effective as a teacher, there are three "loves" that you must develop.

First, you must love *who* you teach. This might seem obvious, but if you want to be an effective teacher, you must love kids! If you are going to teach kindergarten, you have to love spending time with young kids, getting down on the floor with them, welcoming their runny noses and sticky fingers, and seeing the world of wonder through their eyes. If you are going to teach middle schoolers, you have to love spending time with young adolescents, living in a world of mismatched physical and emotional development, dealing with social drama and body odor and bumbling flirtatiousness, and helping them learn to not take themselves so seriously while also taking their very real concerns very seriously. If you're going to teach high school seniors, you have to love spending time with teens who are coming into their own, but still not fully understanding themselves, who have hopes and fears of what is next that sometimes plays out as apathy, or angst, or aggression, and be willing to nudge, encourage, challenge, and disciple them. You have to love the whole range of diversity that will show up in any group of students you get to serve, with their unique mixture of strengths and weaknesses, talents and struggles, joys and concerns. You simply must love kids if you hope to be an effective teacher—not loving students is the barrier to entry for the profession!

Second, you must love *what* you teach. For middle and high school teachers, this might mean just one or two subjects. For elementary classroom teachers, this likely includes a whole range of subjects. For "specials" teachers, this means loving art, or music, or physical education, or the like so deeply that you want to work with a whole range of students in this discipline. For many teachers, this is the thing that drives us: we love a subject so much, we want to help other people learn to love it as well! Think of your most passionate teachers: I suspect their delighted fascination with insects, or *Romeo and Juliet*, or the Pythagorean theorem, or the perfect volleyball serve, or chemical reactions, or World War II, or Greek mythology, or reading lovely picture books might have rubbed off on you, making you feel some measure of wonder and joy as well. Teachers who love their subjects often wind up with students who love those same subjects!

Third, you must love *how* to teach. We should not underestimate the importance of strong pedagogy—the "art and science" of teaching. Consider your own teachers: perhaps you had a teacher who clearly loved students, and obviously loved the subject matter they were teaching . . . and yet were not good at the "teaching" part of the job? Knowing and implementing a variety of instructional strategies is important. Being able to match your teaching techniques to the needs of the students and the demands of the content is critical. Being able to connect your goals to effective teaching strategies, and select effective assessment approaches to judge students' learning is absolutely essential to be effective as a teacher. But the actual work of teaching is complex and nuanced, and it usually doesn't happen in these kinds of discrete chunks of skill areas. Effective pedagogy is multifaceted and usually looks like lots of things happening all at once. For example, as a teacher is teaching a lesson, they are setting learning targets for students, selecting the right strategies for helping students hit those targets, motivating students for learning, managing materials, guiding students towards appropriate behavior, communicating clearly with students, anticipating and addressing misconceptions, and using a variety of assessment strategies to ensure students are on the right track to deep understanding. Teachers who commit to continually honing their skills at teaching because they love how to teach are often the most effective teachers!

These three loves are each important on their own, but in combination they become even more powerful. The most effective teachers ensure that students are learning by integrating their love of who they teach, what they teach, and how to teach. The word "ensure" is a scary word—this is not easy work! But the sum of these efforts is the development of a positive classroom atmosphere where all the students are learning.

And . . . A Fourth Love

These three loves clearly matter a great deal! Any teacher who wants to be effective in the classroom must develop all three of these loves. And what teacher wants to be ineffective in the classroom? No one sets out to become a teacher saying, "I want to be the most mediocre teacher I can be." That is ridiculous, isn't it? I think all teachers have a desire to be effective, to respond faithfully to the high calling they have received.

For Christians in the field of education, I think this prompts a fourth love that we should consider. In addition to loving students, content, and pedagogy, Christian teachers need to love grappling with the way their faith impacts and influences their work. This love is a little different than the first three, and it is, I think, peculiar to Christian educators. All teachers, regardless of their faith perspective, want to rise above the level of mediocrity. But for Christian educators, I think there is something different, something deeper going on here. Every educator is embodying their faith perspective in the work they are doing, whether they are Christian or not.

This might be a new idea for you, so I want to slow down and think this through deliberately and intentionally. Let's carefully consider what it means to be a person of faith, what it means to have your faith influence your work, and what Christian faith in particular might mean for people called to teach.

First, let's consider the fact that everyone is religious.[12] That might sound like a bold claim, but I believe it is true. James K. A. Smith suggests that our particular, individual ways of understanding the world and even our ways of *being* in the world are shaped by our religious beliefs.[13] The things we love shape the way we *are*. This goes far beyond our work life, though it includes our work as well. Faith influences every part of what we do! But this true for all educators, not just Christians. And each teachers' faith life will be embodied in their teaching practice in some ways.

Our worldviews impact our work in both overt and subtle ways. Richard Edlin argues that there is no such thing as "neutrality" for educators; every teacher embodies a belief structure, a religious way of being when they step into their classroom.[14] This is certainly true for Christian teachers; a Christ-centered worldview will impact the things you do as a teacher! The teaching practices of Jewish teachers, Muslim teachers, atheistic teachers, secular humanist teachers . . . fill-in-the-blank with any way of viewing the world . . . all teachers are impacted by the worldview they hold. The way we do our work *must* be influenced by our faith perspective. So, for Christian educators, we cannot *help* but live out our faith perspective in the work we do as teachers. If we love Jesus and are seeking to faithfully follow him, this *must* impact our teaching.

So, at this point, you might be thinking, "I'm a Christian, and a teacher ... I guess that means I am a 'Christian teacher,' right? What difference does that make for the way I do my work on a day-to-day basis?" This is, I think, the KEY question that Christians in education must grapple with—that fourth love, the love of understanding how our faith impacts the way we engage in the work of teaching. *How* we approach the question of faith and teaching matters greatly.

"Christian" as a Noun, an Adjective, and an Adverb

It's time for a little language lesson. Let's go back in time to your elementary school language arts classes and think about grammar and the various parts of speech. I suspect you learned along the way that *nouns* are words for persons, places, or things, and that *verbs* are words that describe actions. *Adjectives* are words that describe nouns, telling what kind of person, place, or thing we are talking about. And *adverbs* are words that describe verbs, telling when, where, or how something happened. There are lots of other parts of speech, but these ones are the ones we will focus on here for a moment.

Now, let's consider the verb "teach." Teaching is an action. Perhaps it's more accurate to describe teaching as a complicated set of actions that happen simultaneously! And because it's an action, teaching is something that someone *does*.

Carrying this forward, let's start thinking about the nouns we could associate with the verb "teach." Who teaches? A teacher, of course! But there are lots of other words we could put in the "noun" spot in a sentence. A *woman* teaches. A *man* teaches. A *professor* teaches. A *mentor* teaches. A *coach* teaches. A *pastor* teaches. A *friend* teaches. Many different people (nouns) can teach.

How about placing the word "Christian" in the noun spot? Can we say, "A *Christian* teaches?" This certainly makes grammatical sense, and I think it makes practical sense as well. Christian is a noun.

In fact, I think the word "Christian" works best as a noun. There is a lovely story in Acts 11:19–30 about the early church, and a group of Jesus's disciples who were living in the city of Antioch. These people were so peculiar, so Christ-like that they were given a name by the people around them: Acts 11:26 says, "The disciples were called Christians first at Antioch." The word "Christian" literally means "little Christ," and this suggests that the people around those Christians in Antioch noticed something about them: they were different from the people around them, and had a label attached to them to illustrate this. It might be that the people of Antioch were trying to insult the Christ-followers by using this term to describe them, as in "Oh look at those cute 'little Christs!' Look how they go around trying to be like Jesus Christ!" I don't know if this interpretation is factual or not, but I think that is a beautiful way for us to think about what it means to be a Christian. Christians are people who stand out from the culture because they follow the way of Jesus. I am a Christian, and by making that declaration, I am saying something about who I am: I love Jesus, and I am striving to be like him, perhaps a little bit more day by day, becoming a little more Christ-like all the time.

So "Christian" clearly functions well as a noun, but we should also take note that it can work as other parts of speech. For example, the word "Christian" can also function as an adjective, describing a noun. We could use "Christian" to describe all sorts of people, places, or things. A *Christian* coach. A *Christian* scientist. A *Christian* carpenter. A *Christian* church. A *Christian* song. A *Christian* book. A *Christian* school.

The word Christian as an adjective can be descriptive, but I do worry sometimes about the way the word could be misinterpreted. For example, what do we mean by a "Christian" school? What makes it Christian? The fact that the school day opens with Scripture reading and prayer? That the curriculum is aligned to a biblical perspective? Is it that the faculty and staff must all be members at Christian churches? Or that the families sending their children to that school are all Christians? Perhaps the school is owned and operated by a church? Maybe that the intended learning outcomes for the school are more than just academic, but also pointed towards shaping effective disciples who love God and follow the servant way of Jesus? There are many possibilities for what the word "Christian" really means when we are applying it to describe a school! Many—or even all—of these descriptors could be rolled together in thinking about what a "Christian school" means. But we don't know for sure, do we? It might just as well be only one of these descriptors. And how about if we apply the adjective "Christian" to a teacher? What does it mean to be a Christian teacher? There is a similar variety of possibilities.

Let me suggest that we instead shift our focus the adverb form of the word Christian. Adverbs typically end in "-ly" to show *how* something happens. Words like "quickly," or "joyfully," or "unfortunately," or "ambivalently" describe the verb that tells the action. So, what if we would use the word "Christianly" to describe actions? "Christianly" might drive us back towards the noun form of "Christian"—being a "little Christ." Maybe doing something Christianly means doing it in such a way that you are illustrating that you are seeking to be like Jesus, to follow his way, to become like him?

Imagination and Teaching Christianly

This whole idea of teaching Christianly is one I've been chewing on for a long time now.[15] Studying to become a teacher at a Christian college as I did, I was encouraged to think deeply about my faith and how it impacts my work as a teacher. And as long as I've been teaching—both in K-12 schools, and now in higher education—I've been working out my faith as part of my teaching practice. But it's not easy work, and it's something I have continued to develop throughout my years as a teacher.

So maybe it's no wonder that I want to continue to discuss the interaction between Christian faith and the teaching profession with colleagues and the future teachers I now work with. In one of the first courses I ever taught for future teachers, our classroom discussion turned to questions about faith and teaching—what we might consider "Christian teaching." I had been wrestling with this for years at that point, so I was intrigued by the fact that my students were the ones who brought up the topic in class that day. It seemed to me that they too felt the pull of this idea—a sense that their faith *should* matter for their work as teachers.

So, I asked the class directly, "Is there such a thing as "Christian teaching? And, if there is, what does it look like?" Most students sort of nodded along in the sense that indicated they thought the answer is "yes, there must be such a thing." But one student spoke up almost immediately, playing the devil's advocate. He seemed almost offended by the idea—as if there was such a thing as a "Christian" way to teach! He asked, "Is there a "Christian" way to do anything? Is there a "Christian" way to smoke a cigarette?" (Hmmm . . . that's a good question!) That got the rest of the class thinking critically about what we *really* mean when we say "Christian teaching" or "Christian education." Class consensus was that there must be such a thing as "teaching Christianly," but they were struggling to articulate exactly what that meant.

They were able to name and describe aspects that they expected to see in Christian schools that seem to illustrate how faith shows up in teaching. They mentioned things like opening the school day with devotions, reading Scripture as part of lessons, praying before lunch and at the end of the school day, having chapel services, studying the Bible as a school subject, and the like. But they also seemed a little dissatisfied with this—is that *all* "teaching Christianly" is? If we sprinkle on a little Jesus, does that make it Christian? It's certainly not that there is anything inherently wrong or *un*-Christian about these things; in fact, we agreed that these are the kinds of things we should expect to happen in Christian schools.

But then, my insightful student who had stirred the pot so perfectly by asking if there was a Christian way to smoke a cigarette asked a Magic Question: "Okay then, can you 'teach Christianly' in a public school?"

The class got a little quiet and reflective. It took a little time for someone to speak up, and the tentative answer was, "I think you *can* teach Christianly in a public school... but I'm not sure what that looks like." The whole class was nodding along; there was clear consensus that you *can*, in fact, "teach Christianly," even in a public-school setting, but no one was entirely clear how that might happen.

After a little further quiet reflection on the part of the class, I suggested we might think of it as a matter of *perspective*: perhaps "teaching Christianly" has more to do with our intent, our approach, our heart. Perhaps "teaching Christianly" means we are striving to be Christlike in our work as teachers? Could it be that straightforward? The future teachers liked that idea, and our conversation turned to other things, but I confess, I kept rolling that idea around in my head.

In the years since that classroom conversation, I've become absolutely convinced that teaching Christianly certainly is a matter of the heart. It is as simple, and as complex as that. It is an easy thing to declare that we are going to follow Jesus in our work but wrestling through the implications of that simple statement will almost certainly change your approach as a teacher from "simply teaching" into something much deeper, richer, and more fulfilling. Let me suggest three aspects we might use to begin imagining the way teaching Christianly takes shape.

First, teaching Christianly means recognizing that Christ is sovereign over all things, including your classroom. Christ's sovereignty is total. He is Lord! Because he rules over all things, Jesus cares about what happens in his kingdom, including your teaching practice. If Jesus is Lord of all, serving him is not a part-time kind of thing; his Lordship means that every part of your life is in service to him! If Jesus Christ is Lord, you must be about building his kingdom, even in your work as a teacher.

Secondly, teaching Christianly means *leading* with the idea that Jesus is Lord. Simply recognizing that Jesus is Lord isn't enough; rather, we should begin by asking, "How does what happens in my classroom *point to* the fact that Jesus is Lord?" This question should prompt us to be intentional about the things we do—and do not do—in actively seeking to build his kingdom in our work as teachers. This shows up in sorts of big and small ways, from the way you frame the curriculum, to the way you place students into groups, to the way you communicate with parents, to the way you write quizzes. You might think of it this way: Jesus cares how you arrange the desks in your room, because even in these kinds of small decisions you are living out your citizenship in his kingdom. If Jesus is Lord, all these sorts of things matter!

Thirdly, teaching Christianly means living out our discipleship day by day. What does it mean to be a disciple? Jesus said it himself: "Whoever wants to be my disciple must deny themselves and take up their cross daily and follow me."[16] This is all-encompassing work! It means using the gifts that God has given to us to the best of our abilities and to his glory. It means we serve God by serving our students. It means, in the words attributed to St. Francis of Assisi, we "preach the gospel at all times, using words when necessary."

These three aspects of teaching Christianly can be done in any school—a public school, a Christian school, a parochial school, a charter school, a home school . . . any school! But it takes dedication and intentionality to live out your faith this way.

This work is not easy, obviously! And it might feel overwhelming—indeed, it should probably overwhelm you a little. But take encouragement: remember that God has called you to this work and remember that God equips those he calls. Yes, teaching Christianly is demanding work. But it is *good* work. It is work we *get* to do. And remember that we do not do this work alone! The good news is that the Holy Spirit is at work in you, nudging you to more faithfully follow Jesus day by day. We may never fully arrive at teaching Christianly as a destination on this side of glory, but we get to keep on growing in our abilities to do this even as we continue to grow in our faith.

Questions for Reflection after Reading

1. Does the idea of "teaching Christianly" (the adverb form) as opposed to "Christian teaching" (the adjective form) change the way you think about the relationship between faith and teaching? Why or why not?
2. What is a new idea that helped expand your imagination?
3. What challenged your thinking, or what question would you like answered?

Chapter 4

Joys and Challenges of Teaching Today
History, Reform, and the Future

Taylor's Journal . . .

Today was one of those days where I realized how young some of my colleagues think I am. We were in the teachers' workroom this morning, and one of my more "seasoned" colleagues was complaining about the topic of our professional development workshop coming up this Friday afternoon. "All these new initiatives our principal is pushing on us—it's ridiculous! As if any of them will stick and make a difference for students' learning."

I started to argue that I thought it could be interesting to learn something new. She turned and looked right at me: "Taylor, you're still too new to this teaching thing, but you'll figure it out someday: what goes around comes around. I've been doing this long enough to know that three years from now, we'll have another professional development workshop that tells us we should be doing exactly the opposite thing that this Friday's expert is saying is the best way to teach. What a waste of everyone's time!" And she turned and left the workroom with me standing there, a little flabbergasted.

Wasn't that a great way to start the day? I guess I'm just wondering now if she's right: is there really "nothing new under the sun?"

Is Teaching Harder Today than It Was in the Past?

I just want to be explicit on one point as we begin this chapter: teaching is hard work! There seems to be a cultural narrative that teachers are sort of glorified babysitters who just kind of take care of kids, keep them safe, and hopefully help them learn something along the way. This view minimizes the profession, obviously. And anyone who has ever served as a teacher will immediately see this is a false narrative! Teaching is a complex, demanding task. This is not meant as a slight to babysitters; caring for children can certainly be demanding in its own right. But teachers have a different office, one with its own set of responsibilities.

I think we might rightly wonder if teaching is more difficult today than it was in the past. As we discussed in a previous chapter, teachers face a variety of challenges, from the students' needs, to parents' demands, to societal expectations, to personal pressures. But are these different than challenges in the past?

I am not sure that the *actual work of teaching* is necessarily more difficult than it was in the past, but the social context of teaching does seem to have shifted over time. Teaching, and school culture overall, exists in a particular societal moment. And because societal beliefs might shift over time, we can—and should—expect that expectations for teachers will also shift over time.

I've heard it said before that the only constant thing in the field of education is that it will always change. That might sound like a cute saying, but there is a lot of truth in it! School culture reflects the broader culture of the society the school is situated within. When societal beliefs and expectations shift, we will see a corresponding shift of culture in schools as well, and with this shift, a change of expectations on teachers. A little exploration of the history of education might help to illustrate this, so let's take a brief look at the history of American education.[17]

Joys and Challenges of Teaching Today

A Brief History of American Education

Let's begin our exploration in the 1800s. By the mid 1800s in the United States, it was generally accepted that education was a public good, and that schools should be supported by taxes. There was also a general cultural expectation that teachers should be prepared as professional educators, and that all children should be expected to attend school. Schools certainly looked different depending on the location. I often picture the one-room schoolhouse from reruns of *Little House on the Prairie* when I think of education in the 1800s: one teacher with students in grades 1–8 all learning together. Perhaps it's no wonder that in that kind of setting the expectations were to master basic skills? The curriculum of such schools was sometimes described as the 3 Rs: "reading, 'riting, and 'rithmetic." In other words, you might be considered educated if you could read fluently, write well, and compute accurately. Other subjects might have also been included but were not necessarily the focus of the teaching and learning. (And if you were the teacher responsible for teaching such a grade range, who could blame you for limiting the scope of the curriculum?)

Culture began to shift over time, however, and by the turn of the twentieth century, the Progressive Era had begun. This era in American history was marked by efforts to end government corruption and emphasize social reforms that would lead to better lives for all Americans in terms of health, economic growth, and general flourishing of people. And so, education began to shift as well. John Dewey was an influential thinker and writer during this time, and while he was teaching at the University of Chicago helped to develop an educational philosophy known as progressivism. Progressivism argues for experiential education that focuses on individual growth and learning. During this period, schools shifted their focus: instead of just emphasizing the 3 Rs, schools began to include more firsthand learning experiences tailored to students' unique strengths and interests rather than only ensuring that students master a pre-determined set of skills. Dewey's ideas were influential, and impacted schooling over the next few decades.

Through the 1930s and 1940s, different schools in different areas may have had more emphasis on the "just the basics" approach of the 3 Rs, or more emphasis on the "student-centered" approach of Dewey's experiential approach. The Great Depression and World War II were life-altering events for most families and communities, and as society grappled with the uncertainty of this period, schools had a similar complicated mixture of ways that they responded to local needs, and thus school culture was again impacted by broader society.

Things collectively shifted, however, with the Soviet Union's launch of Sputnik I, the first man-made satellite to orbit the Earth, in 1957. This was the beginning of the Space Race between the USSR and USA, and a cultural fear in America of losing out to the communists caused a shift of culture in schools. This fear caused a sort of single-minded resolve that manifest in American education: there was a sense of the United States being "behind" the Soviets when it came to math and science and engineering, and so there was a shift of emphasis away from the experiential learning towards ensuring that all students would master basic skills. New strategies for teaching math were incorporated into education with the idea that this would better prepare American students to compete intellectually on the international stage.

But there were more cultural shifts coming. The 1960s and early 1970s saw the rise of the counter-culture movement. Largely inspired by opposition to the Vietnam war and militarism of the United States government, anti-war protestors and hippies became mainstream and had a significant cultural impact. Schools responded by moving again in the direction of more student-centered, experiential learning. Perhaps the farthest point in this cultural educational reaction would be the Open Schools movement of the late 1960s and early 1970s. The basic premise of this movement was that kids would naturally learn if left to their own devices and given space and choice of what they want to do. Imagine a school building without interior walls, with lots of different activities set up, and kids having the autonomy to move around and work on what they feel like working on. Want to paint today? Paint away! Want to do some science? Materials are available. Want to read? There's a whole library in the corner of the learning space. While there were some benefits of this approach, it was difficult for teachers to manage, and some parents began to wonder whether their kids were really learning. These concerns grew over time, and the Open Schools movement ended up being fairly short lived.

By the early 1980s, culture was again shifting. After the economic recession of the late 1970s, many Americans were concerned about the state of the economy, and whether American workforce was able to continue to compete on the global stage. Under President Reagan, the U.S. Department of Education released an incredibly influential report entitled *A Nation at Risk: The Imperative for Educational Reform*. The report begins this way:

"Our Nation is at risk. Our once unchallenged preeminence in commerce, industry, science, and technological innovation is being overtaken by competitors throughout the world."[18] That sounds a little ominous, doesn't it? And schools responded to this shift in culture, shifting away from the experiential and towards a heavy focus on basic skills. The thinking was that American schools needed to ensure that all graduates would be ready to enter the workforce as productive members of society. This economic imperative was a driver for many curricular changes, including the number and types of courses that all high school students should take (such as four years of English, at least three years of math and science, three years of social studies, and learning a foreign language) as well as many other reforms, such as recommending a longer school day and at least 200 school days each year. All these reforms were intended to boost students' abilities to be ready to join the American workforce upon graduation.

This shift was further entrenched in the 1990s with the rise of the standards-based education movement. Throughout the early 1990s, many professional educational organizations such as the National Council of Teachers of Mathematics (NCTM) and the National Council of Teachers of English (NCTE) began developing standards to govern their respective content areas. States were encouraged to adopt these standards—or develop their own—so they would be able to more accurately measure and document student achievement. The goal was ensuring mastery of the content, and this mastery was confirmed by standardized tests. The role of standardized testing was further cemented by President Bush signing the No Child Left Behind Act of 2001, which set specific goals for student achievement—as measured by those standardized tests—by 2014. However, it became clear that many states were not going to be able to meet those goals. So, in the early 2010s, another set of standards was developed, the Common Core State Standards, which were adopted by most U.S. states. President Obama signed the Every Student Succeeds Act (ESSA) into law in 2015, which provided funding to states that adopted the Common Core Standards to further support students in meeting these standards. Part of ESSA is a reauthorization for standardized testing at certain grade levels for language arts and mathematics, to ensure that all students are meeting essential standards for these content areas. All these changes were aimed at strengthening schools and seeking to ensure that every American student had the opportunity to master basic skills and foundational knowledge.

Perhaps you noticed something in this history. Think back to the beginning when I was describing schooling in the 1800s. Remember the curriculum? It was made up of the 3 Rs: reading, 'riting, and 'rithmetic. I find it fascinating that where we are today in our high stakes, high-accountability school culture dominated by standardized testing that the subjects mandated for testing are . . . language arts (reading and writing) and mathematics ("arithmetic.") Throughout all these decades and all the reforms they included, perhaps some things just aren't that different. This reminds me of what the Teacher in the book of Ecclesiastes says:

> What has been will be again,
>   what has been done will be done again;
>   there is nothing new under the sun.
> Is there anything of which one can say,
>   "Look! This is something new"?
> It was here already, long ago;
>   it was here before our time.
> No one remembers the former generations,
>   and even those yet to come
> will not be remembered
>   by those who follow them.[19]

While that might sound like a cynical viewpoint, I think it's worth remembering that the history of education, and of education reform in particular, is almost always a "nothing new under the sun" story. We seem to be on a pendulum swinging back and forth between two poles.

The pendulum of education reform swings between the more curriculum-focused and student-focused ends of the spectrum. As I've laid out this brief history, I've tried to emphasize the way schools were responding to cultural pressures from outside of schools. But I think this history also demonstrates two broad underlying approaches to "doing school." There have obviously been times in the history of American education when the focus was on the content of the curriculum. There also have been times when the clear focus was on students and their needs and preferences. This prompts me to wonder if the truth is somewhere in the middle, if there is some way to emphasize *both* the importance of the curriculum *and* the importance of the learners?

Contemporary Challenges

Considering that pendulum-swing of educational history between the "just the facts," curriculum-centered pole and the "think of the children," student-centered pole, it's worth noting that in contemporary schooling there is a combination of these perspectives. Standards continue to dominate the conversation of the curriculum, and high stakes standardized tests are still a major part of students' experiences in school. But at the same time, a growing emphasis on social and emotional learning has been being infused into schools. More and more schools are hiring social workers to help support students' mental and emotional health. And over the past few decades, schools have become more inclusive: students with physical and learning disabilities, students with behavior disorders, and students who are English language learners are all regularly included in the same classrooms with their typical peers. This means that schools have also hired more specialists who are able to support classroom teachers and provide interventions for students who need them as part of their learning and development.

This is fascinating, because these two approaches are rooted in two very different philosophies of education. Your own philosophy of education can begin to be uncovered by asking, "What is the goal of education?" The way you answer that question reveals something about your perspective on how you view students, how you view the purpose of schools, and what you think schools should look like, what curriculum should look like, what "good teaching" looks like, what assessment should look like, and more.

How do different individuals answer that question? For those on the curriculum-focused end of the spectrum, their answer might be, "The goal of education is to ensure that every student has the opportunity to master the basic skills, essential knowledge, and significant understandings that will allow them to fully participate in contemporary culture." Note that this position has its strengths! There is an emphasis here on equality, and on providing opportunities. Also, there definitely is something compelling about the argument that everyone *should* have at least a basic knowledge about the world and how it works. But there may be some weaknesses to this perspective as well. Some critics would say that different kids need different things, and by forcing everyone to march through the same curriculum we might not actually be serving students well at all.

So, let's contrast this by considering the student-centered end of the spectrum. In contrast, they might answer the question by saying, "The goal of education is to ensure that every student is valued, loved, and celebrated for their own unique talents and gifts, and has the opportunity to develop in a way that results in their personal flourishing." Note that this position too has its strengths! This perspective emphasizes the uniqueness of different kids, and ensuring that school is meaningful, relevant, and accessible to each learner. However, there are potential weaknesses here too. Most looming among the concerns: can we *actually* meet the unique needs of 25 different kids in one classroom?

All of this leads to a complex mixture of different philosophies of education being enacted simultaneously; in one classroom we can see both a curriculum-centered focus as well as a student-centered focus at the same time. This complexity adds to the demands on the teacher: teachers today are expected to *both* ensure that all students meet high standards *and* ensure that all students have their unique learning needs met. What is a teacher to do?

Choosing Joy in Light of your Calling

It might be tempting at this point to throw up your hands and say, "I'm out! Teaching seems too hard. I can't do this!" I hope you won't turn and run so quickly as that. Teaching *is* demanding. That's how I started this chapter if you'll remember: teaching is hard work! But it is *good work*. It is *incredibly important work*. And my hope is that this brief look at the history of education actually is a word of encouragement to you even as you consider the challenges of teaching today.

Most things worth doing demand something of those who do it. This is true of teaching in particular, and this is why I wanted to spend so much time in the opening chapters of this book thinking about what we mean by calling, and being called to teach in particular. Remember that God calls us first to be faithful disciples, to follow Jesus day by day.

For those of us called to teach, we conduct our discipleship throughout our teaching practices. No matter the classroom in which we find ourselves, our first calling is to illustrate that Jesus is Lord. John Van Dyk encourages us to think of living out our calling in this way: "What kind of people are we in the classroom? How do the students see us? Can they see that we love the Lord and want to live our life in service to him? . . . Do I display the Fruit of the Spirit, or just their opposite? Am I loveless, crabby, impatient, harsh, and short-tempered too often?"[20] This is a helpful nudge for me on the days when teaching feels hard. We have an opportunity to demonstrate our love for the Lord through each interaction we have with students, parents, colleagues, and administrators.

Will we do this perfectly? Certainly not. We all fall short. But there is grace here too: Jesus loves us, just as we are. A former pastor of mine used to use a particular way of phrasing this, and it has helped me to keep the right focus: "There is nothing you can do that will make God love you more. There is nothing you can do that will make God love you less. God loves you, right now, just as you are, as much as it is possible for an infinite God to love!"[21] And here is the good news that comes with this truth: we can live a life of joyful obedience to God, because he loves us!

So, is the work of teaching hard? Absolutely. Teaching Christianly may well be the hardest job in the universe![22] But is it *good work*? Without a doubt, yes! And because I am loved by God, I can choose joy in my work as a teacher, every single day. This does not mean there will not be bad days, or hard times, or challenging students, or pendulum swings of education reform. Teaching Christianly is a journey, not a destination. And engaging in the hard, joyful work of teaching is not something we *have to* do . . . it's something we *get to* do in service to the King!

Questions for Reflection after Reading

1. Did the history lesson in this chapter change your impressions of the work of teachers today? Why or why not?
2. What is a new idea that helped expand your imagination?
3. What challenged your thinking, or what question would you like answered?

Chapter 5

Do the Right Thing
Professionalism and Ethics

Taylor's Journal . . .

I had an awful moment at the end of the day Tuesday. I totally lost my cool with the kids. They were being so disrespectful, and nothing I was doing seemed to get them to turn it around. Finally, I got so upset, and yelled, "Will you all just shut up for a minute?" The kicker: I was so angry I threw my pen across the room. I didn't hurt anyone, but I know I felt out of control.

    But it got worse: this afternoon my principal stopped by my classroom. His face was serious as he said, "We need to talk about how you lost your temper in class on Tuesday." I felt my face get hot as he shared that he had two phone calls from concerned parents. And I can totally understand why they would be concerned—my behavior was so unprofessional! I already talked with the students about it today and apologized to them for my bad behavior, but I feel like I have a lot of recovering to do. My principal and I brainstormed some ideas for how to move forward, and I said I'd follow up with those parents who had called. I'm honestly grateful that *he came to talk to me about it, even though it was embarrassing. Ooof . . . this job is so hard because I feel like I have to manage myself so much of the time! Being "professional" isn't always easy.*

Jobs, Occupations, Careers, and Professions

In an earlier chapter we discussed the term "vocation" and found out that it really means "calling." This means that if we describe teaching as our vocation, we are saying that we are *called* to teach, with everything that this implies. But there are other ways to talk about teaching as well beyond naming it as a vocation. People describe teaching as a job, an occupation, a career, a profession.

Are these descriptors all saying the same thing? In common English, we might use any of these words interchangeably. But there is some nuance to each one. A "job" is a task to complete. An "occupation" is something that keeps you busy, something to fill your time, something to keep you . . . occupied. A career usually indicates a long-term work situation, with opportunities to develop and move up the metaphorical ladder in terms of responsibilities—and compensation. And a profession is usually thought of as a particular kind of career path that requires very specialized training or education, such as becoming a doctor, a nurse, a lawyer, a minister, an engineer, or an accountant. But how about teaching? Where does teaching fit in these descriptors?

Let's consider each of these as applied to teaching. Is teaching a job? It can be viewed that way, as there certainly are tasks to be completed on a day-to-day basis. Is teaching an occupation? Teaching will certainly keep you busy! There is always planning, assessment, communication, management, and preparation to do. Is teaching a career? It certainly can be a long-term work situation—for many people who enter this field, it is what they do throughout their working years. And there are opportunities for advancement into new and different kinds of leadership roles, such as becoming a curriculum expert, an instructional coach, a department leader or grade-level team leader, or an administrator, for example. Is teaching a profession? This is a great question, and one that is less easy to answer.

When thinking of teaching as a profession, we should carefully consider what makes a profession "professional." There was a time that teaching was clearly considered a profession by almost everyone. In the past, teachers were often among the most educated people in a community. This is less likely to be true today with many people attending college and studying a wide variety of professional fields. But even with this cultural shift, teaching can still be considered a profession. There truly is specialized training in knowledge and skills that are needed to be effective as teachers, and the truth is that not everyone is equipped to do the demanding work expected of professional educators.

There may be a cultural narrative held by some people that teachers generally function as childcare workers who will ideally help kids learn a few things along the way. What an insult to the passionate, professional teachers who dedicate themselves to mastering the craft of teaching! Teaching is *far* more complex than most non-teachers understand, and the professional preparation required is essential for success. It might be hard for non-teachers to imagine the complexity, because the most effective teachers make the work of teaching look so easy. Maybe it's no wonder that some people think that "anyone can be a teacher," but there is substantial professional preparation that is required.

The preparation to become a teacher is multifaceted and multi-dimensional, but it echoes those three loves we discussed in an earlier chapter: effective teachers need to love who they teach, what they teach, and how to teach. These three loves are illustrated in the different aspects of their professional preparation as well. Professional educators spend significant time learning about the people they will teach; they learn about human development and theories of how people learn, ways to adapt their teaching to meet the needs of a diverse group of students, and strategies for creating an environment where learning can take place. Professional educators spend substantial time and effort developing deep content knowledge in the subjects they teach and learning ways of structuring curriculum so that students will learn. In terms of the actual work of teaching, professional educators spend considerable effort learning various methods of assessing students' learning, developing strategies and habits of mind for planning (from whole-year plans down to daily lesson plans), and mastering a wide variety of instructional techniques and approaches for engaging students in learning. And all of this is just in their pre-service preparation! Pre-service teachers learn both the theory ("book learning") and practice ("hands-on learning") through coursework and fieldwork, which complement each other and give them the opportunity to develop the knowledge and skills necessary to be effective educators ready to join the teaching profession.

Teaching is a profession. Because this is true, teachers have certain expectations to meet, and responsibilities that they must fulfill. In the next section, let's consider some of the attitudes and behaviors that will be exhibited by professional educators.

What Does It Mean to be "Professional" as an Educator?

If you have spent any time at all in a classroom as a student, you have some idea of the work teachers do. There are many aspects of the work of teaching that are very obviously visible: we see teachers asking questions, reading aloud, calling on students, facilitating discussions, assigning work, grading papers, and more. Other aspects of the work of teaching are more invisible to students: planning lessons, writing quizzes, giving feedback on student work, documenting learning, preparing materials, collaborating with colleagues, and engaging in their own ongoing learning and development. All of these are important parts of the work of teaching, and this is certainly not an exhaustive list. But in all these ways, and many more, teachers exhibit their professionalism. In the same way that some parts of the work of teaching are more public and others are more private, some of the attitudes and behaviors that illustrate professionalism for teachers are more visible and others are more invisible.

What might we look for to examine whether a teacher is exhibiting professionalism? Imagine watching a teacher at work and taking note of all the "professional" markers we can notice. We might first notice some obvious physical things, such as dress and grooming. We might notice the way the teacher interacts with students and colleagues, and the way the teacher communicates, both verbally and non-verbally. We might notice things about the learning environment the teacher has created, and the classroom climate. Looking closer, we might notice things about the way the teacher plans lessons, and what teaching methods are being used, and how students' work is evaluated. What do these kinds of things show us about professionalism?

Dress and personal hygiene do matter. Two old sayings come to mind for me when I think about this aspect of professionalism. First, "the clothes make the man." Second, "you never have a second chance to make a first impression." Both sayings are worth considering as we imagine the interactions this teacher will have throughout the school day. What does "professional" dress look like for a teacher? It probably depends on the local culture of the school, and on the kind of work the teacher will do as part of her or his position. Rather than asking, "Should I be wearing a tie?" or "Should I be wearing high heels?" perhaps the right question to ask is, "Is what I'm wearing appropriate for the work I'm going to be doing, and does it help me demonstrate that I take that work seriously?" It might seem silly to worry about what we wear, but people make many snap judgments about people just based on appearances, and this might be a first consideration.

Communication is an essential part of the teaching profession. Almost every part of the work we do as teachers involves interacting with other people, and the way we use both language and non-verbal communication strategies matters greatly. The kind of questions we ask, the way we respond to others, the facial expressions, and the gestures we use . . . all of this communicates a sense of professionalism. Measuring our words carefully will help ensure that people do not mistake our meaning. This is important for teachers; we must keep in mind the position of influence we hold! Speaking gracefully, kindly, and in ways that build others up are all part of professionalism for teachers.

Classroom climate might feel elusive, but there are markers of professionalism here too. Classroom climate might be described as the *feeling* you get from being in the classroom. Does the space feel warm and inviting, or cool and detached? Is it a chaotic environment? Sterile? Overstimulating? There are many factors to consider in the climate of the classroom that indicate a sense of professionalism in the teacher. Many of the smaller scale decisions a teacher makes about the arrangement of the classroom illustrate how they think of their role in that space: how student seats are arranged, what is displayed on the walls and bulletin boards, the level of tidiness (or messiness) that is expected in both teacher spaces and student spaces, and the presence (or absence) of teacher's personal stuff in the room all lend to a particular kind of atmosphere. As you spend time in various classrooms, notice what is on display and what this demonstrates about the teacher's sense of professionalism.

As we look closer, we might start to notice specific "moves" the teacher uses in the work of teaching that can further illustrate their sense of professionalism. This might take a little more imagination, particularly if you are new to the teaching profession. There are a wide variety of strategies teachers might use for planning, for instruction, and for assessment, but there are some principles that cut across this diversity that help illustrate professionalism in practice. A tight alignment all the way through a lesson from setting the targets for learning through the intentionally selected teaching strategies to the planned modes of assessment is one good indicator. Regardless of the content of the lesson or the particular strategies being put into practice, this kind of careful planning is almost certainly an indicator of professionalism. Understanding the value of tailoring teaching methods to the students' needs or the demands of the content is another good indicator of a high level of professionalism. The way a teacher provides feedback on students' work, whether verbally or in writing, is another marker of professional practice. The main idea here is that intentionality in the kinds of teaching moves a teacher chooses to utilize reveals a sense that they are carrying themselves as professional educators.

There are some other, more invisible markers of professionalism that we should consider as part of developing a teacher imagination. Developing reflectiveness, practicing creativity, and a commitment to ongoing learning are all essential aspects of growing in professionalism as well.

Reflection is one of the most important aspects of professional growth for teachers. The work of teaching is busy but making time to think about what is working well (or less well) in the classroom is a key component of professional development. Teachers build reflection into their practices in many ways. Some teachers make a point of taking a few minutes at the end of each day to jot notes on their lesson plans about what they repeat the next time they teach that lesson, as well as things they should do differently. Other teachers journal their ideas about their practice, taking time to inventory successes and make plans for future development. Still others participate in professional learning communities in which they have intentional conversations with fellow teachers about their practices. In each of these cases, the main idea is that teachers are making space to notice what they are doing in their teaching practices and making plans for the future based on these reflections.

Creativity is often viewed as something we either have or do not have. Perhaps part of the problem is that many people equate "creativity" with being "artistic." But this is definition is perhaps lacking, because while artists are certainly creative, the truth is that *all* human beings are creative in some ways. God created us in his image,[23] and one of the ways we reflect what our creator is like is in our own capacity to make things and exercise creativity.[24] To teach is an innately creative activity; the whole idea of designing instruction and developing learning experiences for students is an invitation to creativity. Creativity in teaching is often exhibited through resourcefulness and playfulness—using ideas, tools, materials, and strategies that may have been developed by others in inventive ways. And the good news is that teachers can develop their own creativity by practicing it. Taking small risks in teaching, and learning from how that classroom adventure unfolded, and applying that new learning in the future is a key approach to growing in creativity. Developing creative capacities is almost always a mark of professionalism for teachers.

We never really "arrive" as teachers, but we can certainly always keep getting better at our craft. A commitment to ongoing learning is a hallmark of professionalism in the teaching profession. Professional development opportunities abound for teachers. School-based trainings at the beginning of a new school year or on days set aside for professional development are very common. Workshops and webinars aimed at helping teachers develop their knowledge or skills in specific techniques are also very common. Professional conferences are a great opportunity for networking and learning new approaches to both content and pedagogy. Joining a professional organization or subscribing to a professional journal can also be helpful ways to keep up with new developments in the field of education, or in a specific grade level or subject area. Many teachers continue their professional learning in formal ways by taking coursework towards a further degree. And many teachers today participate in informal professional learning by engaging with other educators through social media and online resources. The essential idea here is that teachers exhibit professionalism through their desire to keep growing and improving throughout their careers.

As we have seen through this section, there are many markers for professionalism in teachers. Some are more obvious and noticeable just by spending time in a teacher's classroom. Others are less tangible and might require a closer look. These behaviors and attitudes taken together illustrate a teacher's approach toward her or his practice, and collectively illustrate an approach to professionalism. But what drives a teacher to act in professional ways? What is motivating these behaviors and attitudes?

A Code of Ethics

When watching a teacher conducting their craft, we can perceive some aspect of their beliefs about their work. We can perceive aspects of their professionalism by their appearance, their speech, the environment they create, and the moves they use in their practice. What is harder to discern is the reasons *why* they are doing these things. What drives the behaviors?

All teachers have some sort of way of orienting their professional work, and we might describe this as their code of ethics. Unless they are an absolute sociopath, every person has some moral sense within them, some sort of inner compass that directs them as they consider the right thing to do in each situation. We might think of a code of ethics that way: what guides us to do the right thing? What principles do we hold that help us know if what we are doing is the right thing to do? Ethical behavior is always a part of professional practice for teachers, and a code of ethics underpins all the rest of our professional practices as teachers.

So, what should we rely on for devising a personal code of ethics? The National Education Association (NEA) has a clear code of ethics for all educators.[25] The NEA's code of ethics is built on two straightforward principles: 1) a commitment to the student, and 2) a commitment to the teaching profession. The NEA's emphasis on being committed to students suggests that teachers behaving ethically will always have students' best interest at heart, that they will seek to treat students with dignity, respect, and care, and will strive to help students succeed and flourish. Schools should certainly promote this perspective! The very purpose of schooling is to educate students, and we should encourage all teachers to work towards the flourishing of all their students. Professional educators must be committed to doing what is best for their students.

At the same time, the NEA's emphasis on being committed to the teaching profession encourages teachers to take pride in their work and seek to elevate the profession in society. This means that teachers should seek to behave respectably and portray themselves well as representatives of the teaching profession. They should be examples of moral character and competence. Teachers should practice confidentiality, and speak well of their colleagues, their students, and the families they serve. These kinds of actions serve to illustrate the professional judgment and high professional standards all teachers should embody. Professional educators must be committed to serving the public that has entrusted them in their positions of authority.

These two principles—commitment to students, and commitment to the teaching profession—are helpful for developing an imagination for the ethical basis of professionalism. Teachers seeking to do what is best for their students will surely exercise professionalism in their decision-making.

Likewise, teachers seeking to elevate the teaching profession will obviously exhibit professionalism in their work to ensure they are perceived as dedicated servants worthy of trust. However useful these principles may be, they are not enough for Christian educators. There is a deeper spiritual component we must consider as part of our teaching imagination!

Professionalism and Teaching Christianly

The whole idea of teaching Christianly is aimed at being a faithful Christ-follower as you conduct your work as a teacher. You might be wondering then what professionalism has to do with following Jesus? I always appreciate John Van Dyk's wisdom about growing in professionalism as a teacher. He asks us to imagine Jesus walking into our school and wonder what Jesus might ask us. Van Dyk says, "Would he ask, 'Are you a perfectly professional Christian teacher? Is this school perfectly professional in all its ways?' No, he probably would not ask these questions, because he knows our situation . . . he would probably ask—even demand: 'But are you *working* at it?'"[26] This is, I think, the key to teaching Christianly all around: not that we "arrive" at teaching Christianly . . . but that we keep working on it.

In terms of professionalism, this means we can keep developing. We can practice professional behaviors, and cultivate a solid sense of personal and professional ethics. These are things we obviously *should* do! But there is one more aspect to professionalism that we should consider if we are dedicated to teaching Christianly that might help us expand our imagination a bit.

The word at the root of "professionalism" is "profess." To "profess" means to declare, to affirm, to make a claim. Think of that: what if "professionalism" for Christian educators is actually about *professing*? In many church traditions, becoming a member of the church involves making a profession. When we profess our faith, we are declaring, "I believe that Jesus is my Savior and Lord, and I commit to following him."

Let's consider this through the lens of teaching Christianly. What if professionalism is a tangible way for us to profess—to declare, to affirm, to claim—that Jesus is Lord? What if our professional practices as Christians in education are the tangible, visible, intentional ways that we are making our profession of faith? What difference does that make for the particular "moves" we use in our teaching?

I have often wondered if someone watching me through my classroom window would be able to tell I am a Christian by observing me teach. I hope that they would be able to tell that I am a *good* teacher, an *effective* teacher by observing my practices. But I am not convinced that being a "good teacher" is the same thing as teaching Christianly. My professionalism might be on display, but the motivations behind those professional practices are what really matter here. My faith in Jesus motivates me!

Our professionalism is an outward expression of the faith we profess. This should prompt some introspection for every teacher: who is really the Lord of your classroom? And how do your professional practices illustrate this?

Questions for Reflection after Reading

1. Does the emphasis on professionalism in this chapter make sense to you? Why or why not?
2. What is a new idea that helped expand your imagination?
3. What challenged your thinking, or what question would you like answered?

Chapter 6

Understanding Your Office
Learning and Leading

Taylor's Journal . . .

I've been thinking a lot lately about power in my classroom. When I think back to that first year of teaching, it's almost funny to think now how fearful I was of my students. Well, I guess I wasn't really afraid of them specifically. I was more afraid that I would lose control of the class and that they would just go crazy. But I also really wanted them to like me, so I tried to be really easy-going all the time. Boy, did that backfire! I was so stressed all year, and I felt like they were walking all over me.

Year two I definitely over-corrected. I came on so strong, and really cracked down on any behavior that seemed like it would threaten my power. In fact, I think they were actually a little scared of me! I didn't enjoy that, and I am pretty sure they didn't enjoy it either.

But it's interesting for me now looking at how my confidence has grown. I don't really think of power as something for me to hang on to—at least, not like I did those first two years. I don't believe in a don't-smile-until-Christmas *philosophy . . . but I also don't think an anything-goes philosophy is okay either, and I like to think that I'm striking a better balance now. I'm much more likely today to try and share power with my students and give them a real voice in what happens in our classroom. As soon as I say that though, I recognize how I still worry about the kids taking advantage of my good graces. I still have so much more room to grow!*

Teaching and Power Dynamics

If you are interested in investigating interpersonal power dynamics, a classroom might be a perfect laboratory. Who has the power in a classroom? You might notice that a particular popular student holds sway over her classmates, or that the chemistry of a group of students is strongly influenced by a core group of leaders—for good or ill! Teachers also exercise power in the classroom of course, and they can wield this power in ways that are helpful or potentially harmful. Sadly, I suspect that most of us can think of a time that a teacher misused their power in a way that left an impression on us. In my own teaching practice, recognizing the power I have in the classroom has been an interesting journey of growth and discovery.

I can confess it now: early in my career, I was very anxious about how I would "keep control" in the classroom. This is a common concern shared by many teachers new to the profession. I found that there were certain places in my classroom where I felt more powerful than others: standing behind my podium was a powerful place; sitting at my teacher desk in the corner of the room was a less powerful place.[27] When presenting to the whole class, I almost always did this from one of those more powerful places, because I found that students responded better when I did. I developed a "teacher voice" that I could use to command the classroom, and this worked fairly well . . . most of the time. Students still did misbehave from time to time, of course. But teaching from power spots and using my teacher voice helped me feel more powerful in the classroom, and I found success as a teacher by using these strategies.

However, while using power spots was helpful in some ways, I found it had shortcomings. I had to call students out from a distance if they were misbehaving, and that meant my classroom had a more authoritarian feel to it. I was unhappy with this, because I remembered how much I disliked some of my more authoritarian teachers in my own experience as a student. So, I began to shift my practice a bit.

I began moving around the room more, even during whole-class teaching. Because I was very concerned about ensuring that students were behaving appropriately, I began working to proactively nip possible misbehavior in the bud. I still used my teacher voice to call students to account, but I also found that lowering my voice to almost a whisper could capture students' attention in a way that booming over them did not. At the same time, I learned to use my physical presence to help keep students on track by standing near individuals and groups of students who seemed to be likely to get off track. Proximity mattered, and I was better able to address concerns in a more personal way before their behaviors got out of hand without embarrassing students in front of the whole class.

As I continued to gain experience as a teacher, I shifted my thinking from focusing on managing student behaviors toward building relationships. As this shift happened, I also noticed that I gravitated towards different spots in the classroom. I often began class at the door, welcoming students into the room. I was as likely to perch on top of my podium as to stand behind it, or sit on the corner of my teacher desk instead of sitting behind it. I discovered I could lecture from anywhere in the room and was much more likely to roam around and bounce back and forth in my interactions—sometimes with individual students and sometimes with the whole group, even during a whole-class presentation. I would sometimes stand in the back of the classroom while students were at work, or roll around the room in my desk chair to interact with individuals. When they had individual questions, I learned to come right alongside them, crouching down so we would be at eye level with each other. I discovered that if I sat down on my stool instead of standing at the podium when asking questions to the class, they become much more likely to engage in real discussion rather than just answering my questions. These were all small tweaks that happened over time, and not all at once. But one day I realized how rarely I stood in my former power spots anymore unless I needed to get the whole class's attention. This caused me to really reflect: had I abdicated all my power in the classroom?

This shift from authoritarian management practices to a more relational approach to teaching illustrates something about the nature of power, I think. All teachers have power in the classroom, power that derives from the authority of their position. But the way teachers use the power they have varies greatly! As I have developed as a teacher, I have found that sharing power with students—by moving among them, sitting down with them, getting down to their eye-level—has not decreased my authority in the classroom. But it definitely has changed the way I interact with students, and the way the classroom feels for both them and for me as their teacher. Authority and power are linked, but they are not the same thing.

Office Consciousness

I will suggest that our authority as teachers comes from the *office* we hold. That might sound strange at first, because we often think of an "office" as a place rather than a role. But if you are picturing an office as a place, perhaps it makes sense to think of the *place* as just where the authority of a *role* is exercised? When you go to the doctor's office . . . you are headed to the place where the doctor does their work, the place where they exercise the authority of their position. The same could be said of visiting an accountant's office, or a lawyer's office, or a pastor's office, or even the principal's office in a school: these locations are where people who have a particular role to play carry out parts of the responsibilities they have because of their authority. While teachers might not have a physical office you can visit, they *do* have an "office" role to play, because they too have "official" responsibilities, and the authority that comes with them.

When we speak of the teacher's office this way, we are thinking about the official work teachers do. When you sign a teaching contract, this is symbolic of something very important happening: you are assuming an office, with official rights and responsibilities. There is an associated authority that comes with this official position. We become "officebearers," individuals who are granted authority to teach, carrying out our responsibilities within appropriate limits. Accepting the office of teacher means a recognition that you are equipped with the knowledge, skills, and dispositions to carry out the tasks associated with that office. And, for Christian teachers in particular, a consciousness of our office is essentially important. We view ourselves as being called by God himself into the office of teacher! And teaching Christianly means keeping our office—and the associated authority we bear—in mind through a sense of office consciousness.[28]

Being an office-conscious teacher should affect the way we think about power in the classroom. What is it that authorizes me to exercise power in the classroom? Is it just because I'm bigger than my students? Because I'm older than my students? Because I'm more educated? These may all be true, but this is not where our classroom power comes from.

Our real power in the classroom flows out of the legitimate authority that comes from our office as teachers. This authority certainly does carry power with it. But the source of that power is not in the person, it rightly flows out of the office of the teacher.[29] Think back to the "power spots" I mentioned in my classroom. When I was a young teacher, I needed to stand behind my podium to feel powerful—it wasn't anything about me personally being in that spot that made me powerful. It was just a way of exercising the authority that came with my office as a teacher. As I grew and developed as a teacher, I found I could exercise that same authority from many different locations around my classroom. I could share power with my students, empowering them to be active participants in their own education, while still guiding and leading them through the authority I held because of my office.

If we are dedicated to teaching Christianly, office consciousness helps us understand the particular role we play. We are authorized to do our work through the authority of God himself! God calls us to the work, equips us for what he calls us to do, and empowers us to act with the authority in the office we occupy. Will we always do this perfectly? Unfortunately, the answer is no. But carefully considering and understanding the nature of the office we are called to serve within will open our eyes and expand our imagination what is actually happening when we teach.

In the rest of this chapter, let's explore three aspects of the teaching profession that make teaching challenging, but also fulfilling, particularly when viewed through and office-conscious lens: the public/personal nature of teaching, working towards mastery, and developing as a leader.

The Public/Personal Nature of Teaching

It seems to me that everyone believes they understand what teachers do, even if they have never served as a teacher. Perhaps it's no wonder that everyone has an opinion on the teaching profession because there have been aspects of the profession on display for them every day they spend in the classroom. And students certainly *do* have some ideas of the work of teaching. Teaching is a very public profession in this regard: we always do part of the work in front of people.

The public aspects of the teaching profession are often the parts teachers find most exhilarating . . . and the most daunting. Interacting with students has simultaneously been both the most joyful and the most demanding part of the profession for me. This is because when I am teaching, I am engaging with real human beings, with real emotions, and life experiences, and motivations that may or may not line up well with my lesson plan for the day. All my knowledge of student development, and learning theories, and pedagogy, and strategies for engagement are hovering just over my shoulders, and it comes together in a real space as I interact with real people. Teaching is not for the faint of heart! This is very public work, and subject to public scrutiny by the very people who are simultaneously the recipients and the spectators of all my planning and preparation: the students.

When a teacher steps in front of the class, there is a sense in which we are putting ourselves on display. Students rarely see all the preparation and careful deliberation teachers put into the work that readies them to step into that space where they engage with students. We teachers have a whole private universe behind our interactions with our students, with our own emotions, experiences, and motivations. Remember in a previous chapter when we considered *identity* and *integrity* as a teacher? You bring your whole self into the work! Thus, teaching truly is a very personal vocation: if we don't put ourselves into the planning, preparation, and execution of a learning experience with students, we are reducing the beautiful work of real teaching to mere technique.

The public/personal nature of teaching is one of the most difficult parts of the profession that we all must navigate. How much should I tell students about my life outside of school? What is an appropriately professional relationship? Can I be friendly with my students without trying to be their friend? If things go off the rails in the classroom, will students think less of me? When students say or do things that hurt my feelings, should I let them know? Can I joke around with students, or will this cause them to lose respect for me? What do I do if I run into my students outside of school—am I still their teacher there too? There are many questions rolled up in this public/personal nature of teaching, and there often aren't easy answers.

But here is where bringing office-consciousness into the conversation might help give us some guidance for ways to think about the role we play in our students' lives. In the office of teacher, we have a responsibility for the formal education of the students entrusted to our care. Our authority stems from our office, and our power in the classroom must be used in accordance with that position of authority. What this means in practice is that we must be mindful of the way we engage with students. Professionalism matters, behaving ethically matters. This might make it seem that we should hold our students at arm's length, ensuring that we don't get "too close" to our students in a way that would diminish our authority. But there is also an appropriate and healthy way that we can disclose parts of ourselves to students, and this can help us more authentically connect to our students in a way that enhances the authority of our office.

Think of the best teachers you ever had. What was it that made them so effective? It probably wasn't just their mastery of the content, or their excellent pedagogical skills—though these are definitely important. I suspect that the best teachers you had found ways of navigating that line of appropriate self-disclosure that maintained their professional position, but also made them real human beings. This is not easy work! But keeping in mind our office as teacher can give us some guidance into this. For example, I recommend that teachers follow what I call the Golden Rule for Teachers, which I frame as, "Never ask your students to do something you are unwilling to do yourself." Here is one way to picture what this could look like in practice: if I ask my students to share a story from their lives outside of school, I will first tell a tale from my own life to illustrate. This allows me to practice the authority that comes with my office as teacher in a way that appropriately shares something about myself, helps build connections with the students, and strengthens their sense that I am a real human being.

Teaching is simultaneously very public work, and intensely personal work. While these two impulses can seem to be at odds with one another, viewing the work through an office-conscious lens can help us to do the public work with heart and soul, while also bringing our personal selves into the work in an appropriate way.

Mastery Is an Asymptote

When I think back to my first years as a teacher, I sometimes think it would be wonderful to be able to go back in time . . . to apologize to those students I taught in the first years of my career. I was not a very good teacher when I started in this profession! Oh, I had good days, and days when my lessons worked out just as I had planned them. And, honestly, I had more successes than failures—if this was not the case, I suspect I would not still be teaching today. But teaching can seem like an arcane art with a steep learning curve, particularly to those new to vocation.

I do think that teachers today are generally better prepared for entering the profession than I was; we keep learning about how people learn, and this certainly helps novice teachers to be more fully equipped to begin their own classroom practices. But there are some things that you can only learn by doing, and I believe teaching is one of those things.

I believe the real challenge for learning to be a teacher is the recognition that we must never stop learning! I will be bold enough to say it: if a teacher is unwilling to admit that they need to keep learning, perhaps they should no longer serve as a teacher. We never really "arrive" as master teachers; we can always get better.

When I think back to the mistakes and missteps I made in my first few years of teaching, I can see just how much I learned in those early days. How steep the learning curve was in my first years! I am so grateful for wise colleagues who mentored me through, and an administrator who supported and encouraged me to keep trying new things, and to build on my successes. Year one was very demanding, but I was successful in many ways. My students learned . . . and I learned a lot as well. Year two was better for me, as I was working to fix all the things that felt a little broken after year one and finding more success with both students' engagement in my classroom as well as my own growth as a teacher. Year three was even better, and I felt like the steep curve was beginning to level off as I grew in confidence in my abilities to help my students connect with the content, to plan effective lessons, and to manage challenging student behaviors.

Over the next few years, I continued to refine my teaching practice through intentional reflection. I became more effective at planning lessons by examining on the places where my lessons went a little sideways and changing my plans to mitigate these before it happened in class with students. I became a more grace-filled teacher by reflecting on the places where my classroom management attempts went off the rails, and discussing them with a trusted colleague, exploring ideas for how I could do better. I became a more engaging instructor when I explored the ways that small-scale risk-taking in my pedagogy paid off and began to take some more daring pedagogical risks as a result. I became a more thoughtful assessor when I considered the gaps between my beliefs and practices, and began shifting my strategies for evaluating students' learning to align more closely to what I actually believe about who my students are. These were perhaps more incremental changes to my practice rather than some of the big ones I made in the first few years, but changes nonetheless.

And as I've persisted in my practice as a professional educator, I've continued to reflect, and read, and research, and use the things I'm learning to refine my practice. I haven't "arrived" as a teacher, and I don't think I ever will on this side of heaven. But I keep chasing mastery and keep on learning and growing.

I have come to think of mastery in teaching as an asymptote.[30] In mathematics, an asymptote is a line that a curve approaches. When we draw the graph of the curve, it gets closer, and closer, and closer to the asymptote line. The curve might come infinitesimally close to the asymptote, but it never actually intersects the line. This is the concept of a "limit" in mathematics, right? As x approaches infinity, y gets closer and closer and closer to the line . . . but never *quite* reaches it. And this is what happens for us as teaches as well: we definitely can keep getting better at teaching the longer we practice it, particularly if we are working reflectively, and desiring to keep learning and growing. But mastery is an asymptote: a line we will never cross, at least not on this side of heaven.

If that is true, shouldn't we just despair and stop trying to master the craft of teaching—and particularly teaching Christianly? Let me offer this encouragement: this is another place where viewing the work of teaching through an office-conscious lens can be helpful. The authority of our office as teachers suggests that we have a responsibility to wield that authority wisely. Growing in wisdom is then essential, and one of the best ways to become a wiser, more authoritative teacher is to keep learning. Reflection and collegial conversations are some of the best ways to keep growing and learning as a teacher. Your office demands it; you have a responsibility to the students you serve to not stagnate. Instead, you have the opportunity to consider your practice as an opportunity for growth. Reflect on what is working well . . . and less well. Capitalize on your strengths. When you discover growth areas, commit to learning more about them, and put what you learn into practice. Take small risks, learn from them, and build on successes. Remember that God has called you to this office, and let's not forget that he equips us for the work he calls us to do![31] In response to the joyful challenge of teaching Christianly, let's commit to continue learning, to keep growing, to work towards mastery as a way of living out our discipleship.

Understanding Your Office

Becoming a Whimsical Leader

There are a few events that happened in my classroom that are absolutely seared into my memory, because they were so formative for the way I think of myself as a teacher. One of these occurrences happened during a seventh-grade science class. I was a seventh-grade homeroom teacher, and that year I had an amazing group of students—the sort I could ask almost anything of, no matter how crazy it might seem at first, and they would grab on to the idea and run with me. But when they came into my classroom for their science class that afternoon, I could tell something was going on. They seemed furtive, shooting glances back and forth at each other. I wasn't sure exactly what was happening among them; had something happened in the lunchroom? Out on the playground during recess? Was it middle school drama about to burst into our lesson on Newton's laws of motion?

Despite my apprehension, I launched into my lesson. The students seemed to settle down and start participating in the lesson I had planned. They answered questions I asked and took notes on my lecture on forces and acceleration. But I could tell there was still an anxious energy in the room, a feeling of anticipation for . . . *something*.

And then it happened. Twenty minutes into class, one young lady got out of her seat and laid down on the floor. She did not seem to be in distress, or feeling ill, or anything like that. While I was thinking about how best to respond, another young lady got out of her seat on the other side of the room, and lay down as well. About five seconds after that, a young man in the front of the room slid out of his seat and joined them on the floor. And five seconds after that, two more were on the floor. Within a minute, most of the students in the classroom were laying down on the floor, trying to keep straight faces. As I looked around the room at the few students still in their desks who had a mixture of apprehension in their eyes and the hints of grins at the corners of their mouths, and I said, "Well, we might as well join them, right?" I lay down on the floor in front of the classroom, and continued my lecture while laying with my hands behind my head. The whole class broke down in a roar of laughter—myself included—and some students began shouting, "She was right! She was right!"

Once the laughing began to subside, we sat up and I got the story from them. My good friend who taught English classes down the hall had been trying to define the word "whimsical" for students in their literature class that morning. She had used me as part of her definition for the word—my way of being in the classroom was "whimsical." (I took delight in hearing that from my students!) And so, they had concocted a plan with my colleague's inspiration: a way of testing their theory that I was indeed a "whimsical teacher." Twenty minutes into class, they would start getting out of their seats to lay down on the floor. My colleague was convinced that I would join them on the ground and keep teaching my lesson—exactly what happened! She had promised to take the blame if things went sideways with me in class, and the students agreed to take the risk. They even plotted out who should lay down first, not one of the "naughty" kids in the class, but one of the sweetest, meekest young ladies in the group, which would throw me off. (They were right—it did!) And now I had the explanation for their odd behavior at the beginning of class: they were not sure if they were going to go through with their plan or not, but definitely wanted to. We were all glad that they had the courage to go through with it—even me. I directed them back to their seats, and we continued to chuckle about it, even as I worked back into our lesson for the day.

It is a day I will never forget, and one that caused me a lot of reflection on the nature of power and authority in the classroom. In all seriousness, what would happen if all students in your class suddenly get up out of their seats—whether in playfulness . . . or in revolt? What power do you have to stop them? Here again, let's consider an office-conscious lens on the authority that we hold as teachers. As teachers, we have a responsibility to provide leadership in the classroom; this is one of the primary ways we exercise the authority of our office. But how do we lead? I think there are multiple ways that leadership can manifest in the classroom.

Was I leading when I got down on the floor with my students? It might not seem like it at first glance, but let's think through this scenario. There were several factors to consider in this case. First, consider that I had been teaching for eight years at this point. I was confident enough in my pedagogical skills by that point to flex my lessons based on how students were responding. Earlier in my career, I might have been quicker to snap into action to mitigate what seemed like misbehavior, rather than approaching this situation with curiosity. Add to this the fact that I had a great rapport with this group of students; we had a healthy mutual trust that we had developed, and the chemistry of the group was such that I was able to respond playfully with them while still maintaining an appropriate professionalism. Without these two key developments, I do not think I would have responded quite so whimsically in the moment. But was I *leading* in that moment?

We might best think of leadership—when viewed through the appropriate authority of the office of the teacher—as conducting students towards flourishing. There are times that we need to be more directive in our leadership, and there are times we need to be more responsive. By directive I mean that the teacher needs to give clear and specific guidance to students to ensure they will conduct themselves in a way that results in flourishing. By responsive, I mean that the teacher needs to keep the specific needs of individuals—and the group as a whole—in mind in the way they respond moment by moment. Directive and responsive leadership are not mutually exclusive; these actually go hand in hand. In my whimsical laying down on the floor, it might seem that I was only being responsive to the situation. While I was responding to the immediate situation, I was still able to direct that classroom experience, but this was largely due to the relationships I had intentionally built with students up to that point. Our laughter together was evidence of students' flourishing, as was the fact that we were able to get back to the lesson I had planned, and still meet the learning targets for that day.

Leadership in teaching isn't always about being up in front, though that is certainly part of leading. It also involves the planning and preparation that we put into creating an environment where students will learn, and the way we plan for engagement with both the curriculum and their fellow human beings. We cannot always control students, and, in fact, our power in the classroom might sometimes feel tenuous at best. But the authority we have from our office as teachers empowers us to lead in the classroom. We must take this responsibility seriously, and develop our practices for wielding classroom power with care and concern.

Questions for Reflection after Reading

1. How did you feel about the depiction of power in the classroom in this chapter? Did it resonate with your experiences in classrooms? Why or why not?
2. What is a new idea that helped expand your imagination?
3. What challenged your thinking, or what question would you like answered?

Chapter 7

Jesus Loves the Little Children
Learner Development

Taylor's Journal . . .

I had an interesting conversation in the parking lot yesterday afternoon with Janae, who teaches second grade. She was talking about how crazy it is when you think that the kids coming into her class at the beginning of the year are basically first graders. And then, when they leave at the end of the year, they are third graders. I had never really thought about it that way before: kids really do grow and change a LOT in one year of school!

This has me thinking about my own students, and the ways they are growing up. It happens soooooo slowly that I can't really notice it on a day-by-day basis. But I've been teaching long enough now that when I see kids I taught even just a few years ago, they seem SO grown up now! I guess I shouldn't be surprised by that; it's literally how God created us to be. We all grow and change. I guess I'm just feeling privileged today that I get to have a hand in shaping the people they are growing up to become. What a blessing!

Jesus Loves the Little Children

"If You Don't Love Kids . . . "

When my kids were little, my wife and I taught them the song "Jesus Loves the Little Children." It's a song my own parents sang with me when I was little, and while the original lyrics I learned as a child have some subtly racist undertones, I love this revised version that I have since learned:

> Jesus loves the little children,
> All the children of the world.
> Every color, every race,
> All are covered by his grace.
> Jesus loves the little children
> Of the world!

And Jesus certainly does love children! There are several stories in the Gospels depicting Jesus spending time with children and making time and space for them. In Luke 18 Jesus famously says, "Let the little children come to me, and do not hinder them, for the kingdom of God belongs to such as these. Truly I tell you, anyone who will not receive the kingdom of God like a little child will never enter it."[32] Jesus is capturing something here about the way children receive gifts: hands open, faces full of delight—and we all should be like that when think about his kingdom. And Jesus welcomes children to come to him, both actual children, as well as all of us who recognize and receive with our hands wide open the gift of grace he offers.

Another of my favorite moments of Jesus with children is recounted in Matthew 18, where we find Jesus's disciples arguing about who is the greatest in the Kingdom, and Jesus calls a child to come and stand among the squabbling disciples. Jesus says,

> Truly I tell you, unless you change and become like little children, you will never enter the kingdom of heaven. Therefore, whoever takes the lowly position of this child is the greatest in the kingdom of heaven. And whoever welcomes one such child in my name welcomes me.[33]

These stories of Jesus and the children certainly resonate with teachers because we too love kids! In fact, not loving children and young people is probably a barrier to entry for the teaching profession: if you don't enjoy spending time with kids, this profession is almost certainly not going to be a good fit for you.

In a previous chapter we explored the idea of the different loves we must have to become effective teachers, and the first was loving *who* we teach. In this chapter and the next we'll explore a bit about how our students are created to be and develop our teaching imaginations about how we can engage well with those who we teach.

A Biblical Anthropology: Created in God's Image

"Anthropology" is the study of human beings. Anthropology is usually thought of as a social science involving the study of various cultures and the histories of different people groups. Culture-making is certainly an important part of being human! But we could also think biologically about our make-up as human beings, or psychologically about the way human beings think and feel, or sociologically about how individual humans engage and interact within communities they are part of. There is a whole branch of philosophy devoted to understanding humanity, and how we think about what it means to be human. And thinking theologically, we can consider the way human beings respond in faith and express their spirituality in their day-to-day lives. Human beings are certainly complex, and there is plenty for us to consider here! Teachers need to become amateur anthropologists and carefully consider their students as human beings.

For teachers, understanding our students is an essential part of being able to help them learn. When I interact with my students, I am enacting an anthropology: I am embodying my beliefs about who they are created to be. We should not take this lightly! Our beliefs about our students will play out in our teaching practices in both overt and subtle ways. So, who are our kids we teach? What do we know about them?

There are several pieces of Scripture that we should consider for developing a biblical anthropology regarding our students. Taking these together will help us better understand who they are, and how they are created to be.

Let's begin at the beginning. In Genesis, in the very first chapter of the Bible, we read of God's creative power at work, culminating in his creation of human beings. Genesis 1:27 tells us,

> So God created mankind in his own image,
>   in the image of God he created them;
>   male and female he created them.[34]

What does it mean that we are *created in God's image*? Theologians have argued about this for centuries, and there are many different interpretations of what it means to bear God's image. I have embraced the idea that being an image-bearer of God means that human beings *reflect what God is like*. Think of looking at yourself in a mirror. The image you see in the mirror is not *you*, it is a reflection of you. Your reflection looks like you and does what you do. In the same way, as image-bearers of God, human beings reflect what God is like: we have capacities and abilities and characteristics that reflect God. God is the creator; human beings reflect this in our capacity for creativity. God is love; human beings reflect this in our loving actions. God is wise; human beings reflect this in our capacity for wisdom and reason. God is just; human beings reflect this in our actions that bring justice and mercy. To be clear, human beings are *not* God, in the same way that my reflection in the mirror is not me. We are not totally God-like; he is omnipotent, omniscient, omnipresent, and human beings are not—and cannot be—those things. But as image-bearers of God himself, we reflect what God is like. This truth should guide us in the way we interact with our students, and it should even inform the way we look at our students: they too are created in God's image!

Moving ahead just a few verses in Genesis 1, we read, "God saw all that he had made, and it was very good."[35] Throughout the opening chapter of Genesis there is a refrain that God declares the things he creates as "good," and then, after creating human beings, God declares the totality of his creation as "very good." This is an important truth for us to remember: God's creation—including his image-bearers—is *good*! God does not make junk; God makes beautiful things. Human beings, our students included, are created *good*.

Sometimes it can be hard to see the goodness in human beings, because though we certainly are created good, we also are sinful. Genesis 3 tells the story of the fall, and Adam and Eve, as representatives of the whole human race, disobeyed God. In their sin, all of creation was tainted by sin, and while we can still discern God's good design, sin has twisted everything.[36] Our students then, too, are affected by sin—even from the time they were conceived—and the effects of the fall incline them toward doing evil.[37] The apostle Paul bluntly captures this thought, saying, "There is no one righteous, not even one; there is no one who understands; there is no one who seeks God."[38] But this is a crucially important point to keep in mind: in a biblical view of our students, while human beings *are* sinful, they are not *absolutely* sinful. They still reflect God's image![39] And, as image-bearers—fallen and sinful though they certainly are—they are worthy, valuable, and lovable. And here we have the dilemma: all human beings are created in God's image, and all human beings are totally held captive to sin. What can be done?

Thanks be to God; Jesus came to save the day! Christ's redeeming work breaks sin's hold over creation. Just as Adam and Eve's sin brought the curse of sin crashing down on every part of creation, so Jesus's death and resurrection brings healing and restoration for all things.[40] The good news here is that this means human beings, our students included, are redeemed, bought back from bondage to sin. The possibility of new life has come in Jesus; we have the hope that everything wrong can—and will!—be made right again.

We are living in the in-between time now. Christ's redeeming work has been accomplished, breaking the power of sin. But until he comes again, evil is still at work in this world. It is like we are living through a wartime between Jesus and the forces of evil. Jesus has already won the decisive battle—the war has been won. But there is still the mopping-up operation underway, and the forces of evil are still attacking, though their doom is sure and already spelled out.[41] We can see this in our students too: their sinful human nature will still rear its ugly head from time to time. (Perhaps even daily!) But even in the face of evil's attacks there is hope for full restoration. It is important for us to remember that we cannot save our students; only Christ can do this work of redemption, and his work is already done. But as redeemed sinners ourselves, God calls us to action, being agents of restoration in a broken world. And our students too, redeemed sinners that they are, can work towards the restoration of all things. We all, teachers and students alike, will do this imperfectly, as we are all still touched by sin and in the process of being made holy. The apostle Paul captures this beautifully, saying, "all have sinned and fall short of the glory of God, and all are justified freely by his grace through the redemption that came by Christ Jesus."[42] We humans are broken by sin, but we are also being restored by God's grace through Jesus.

For those seeking to teach Christianly, this biblically-informed anthropology gives us some guiding principles for how we engage with our students. First, we must continuously remember that our students are image-bearers of God himself! This means that we must recognize that they are creative, talented, gifted, and full of the potential that is in God's good design. There may be days this is difficult to keep at the forefront because students *will* sometimes behave badly. But we must not lose sight of the fact that God does not make junk—his creation is *very good*.

Secondly, we must continuously remember that despite being God's image-bearers, our students are sinful. If being an image-bearer means students reflect what God is like, we must recognize that the mirror is cracked, smudged, and tarnished. In practice, this means that students will need correction, and discipline. Perhaps this is a good time to remember though that the word *discipline* shares a root with the word *discipleship*. Our discipline of students must be corrective and restorative, not punishment. Discipline should point students in an orientation towards discipleship.

Third, we must keep focus on the kingdom of God, and our work as teachers should point to Christ's lordship over that kingdom. Our interactions with students should clearly illustrate our belief that Jesus is Lord. We must act with care, kindness, compassion, patience, and self-control. It is true that Jesus loves the little children, and our actions toward the students entrusted to our care should be modeled on the love and grace he embodies.

Knowing who our students are, and how they are created to be informs our work as teachers. We are tasked with an incredible privilege: fostering the learning, growth, and development of children and young people. We know that we will not always do this perfectly, but this is the high calling we have received!

Looking for Patterns

So far in this chapter we've been exploring the broad strokes of a biblical anthropology, a view of who our students are as fallen, redeemed image-bearers. This has, I hope, given the context for thinking more specifically about how students are created to grow and develop. Let's intentionally consider how knowing how students have been created materially influences the way we interact with groups of students.

Think back over your school experiences. Can you remember times where you felt like your teachers were treating you "too young?" Maybe you were in seventh grade, and you felt like the activities you were doing were too childish? Or maybe as a high school student you wanted to say, "Come on, teacher . . . we aren't in middle school anymore!" Or perhaps you felt the opposite: that your teachers' expectations for you were too high? That feeling of "I know you think I should be able to understand this, but I just don't get it at all!" is a terrible one as a student.

As teachers, we need to take our students' development into account, and ensure that our teaching is developmentally appropriate for the learners we have in our classrooms. Kindergartners are at a different developmental level from students in grade 2, who are different from students in grade 4, and so on. Recognizing this is a first step, and an entry point for expanding your imagination as a teacher.

Think of it this way: there are some clear developmental markers that we watch for in babies to see if their growth and development is on track. While there are certainly individual differences, there are some clear patterns of development that we can notice and name. Most babies learn to recognize faces and begin to smile at around two months. Around four months, babies become aware of their hands, and begin to try and use their hands to grab onto toys when you hand them one. Most babies learn to "talk" back and forth with other people by taking turns making noises, and can sit up by themselves by six months. By nine months, most babies are learning to scoot around or crawl. And by one year, most babies are beginning to pull themselves up and start taking their first steps, start saying their first words ("mama" and "dada" are common), and waving "bye-bye." Do all babies develop at exactly the same pace? No. But, these are common patterns to look for, and illustrate what typical development looks like.

These kinds of patterns continue throughout childhood, adolescence, and young adulthood, and we can describe what "typical" development for kids at a particular grade level or age looks like. It's important to keep in mind that individuals will vary, but at the same time, these patterns of development generally hold true. And the key idea is this: recognizing developmental markers for the age group you teach can help you too better respond to the needs of the students you serve.

Developmental Domains

What kind of developmental markers are there? Well, there are multiple developmental domains that we can consider. Let's briefly consider several of them here.

Physical Development

Students' physical development is perhaps the most immediately obvious developmental domain. As kids get older, they generally grow physically larger; they get taller, heavier, and their body shapes change. This physical growth in size is a product of bone and muscle development, which typically occurs steadily through childhood and is punctuated by a burst in adolescence. At the same time, further physical development beyond simply growing larger is brought about by the effects of hormones, which influence other internal and external physical changes at different points, particularly at puberty. And along with this growth and bodily development, there are also typical functional changes throughout childhood and adolescence, including improved hand-eye coordination and enhancement of fine motor skills over time.

Cognitive Development

While students' bodies are developing, so are their minds. Cognitive development is the development of thinking capacities, and students at different age levels have different capabilities. Generally speaking, younger children tend to think more concretely. This means that actual objects they can observe and hold in their hands are often beneficial. This is why children's museums are designed for hands-on learning; the concreteness of getting their hands physically active fosters their understanding. But as they grow up, students develop more abstract reasoning abilities. Concrete learning experiences are still certainly valuable, but they are also more able to reason about things they may not have experienced firsthand. Along with these kinds of thinking abilities, students also typically develop abilities to see things from the perspective of others, giving them deeper empathy for their classmates. They also usually develop greater impulse control, which makes them less reckless, and more self-controlled. These cognitive developments have important implications for learning, of course!

Metacognitive Development

While students' cognitive abilities are developing, they also develop the ability to think about their own thinking. This "thinking about thinking" is called metacognition, and metacognitive development is an important aspect for reflection, goal setting, and self-analysis. Students can learn strategies to help them study and learn about their own habits and preferences for how they engage new ideas and how they do their schoolwork. The ability to analyze past performance and use this information to further learning develops over time, and teachers can help this process by giving students reflection prompts and providing feedback to them. The fact that

God has created our brains with the capacity for us to think about our own thinking is truly marvelous!

Linguistic Development

While students are minds are developing cognitively and metacognitively, they are also developing their capacity to use language in increasingly sophisticated ways. Linguistic development begins in infancy and continues at a rapid pace throughout the pre-school years. Typical students come to school with the ability to communicate effectively using language, but their linguistic development goes on throughout their elementary years and even into adolescence. As humans use language for almost every aspect of their lives, fostering linguistic development is an essential part of teachers' work with students at every grade level.

Emotional Development

Another key part of our development as human beings is emotional development. We are emotional beings from the time we are born, and our development in this domain continues throughout our entire lives. We feel things deeply, and we should remember that joy, sorrow, disgust, surprise, rage, regret, fear, and more are all normal responses to the events of our lives. As children mature, they develop the ability to identify their feelings and describe how they are feeling. By adolescence, most kids can not only tell how they are feeling, but also why they are feeling that way. Along the way, most of us learn to restrain our responses to our emotions. While it is absolutely essential to still feel feelings—we are created as emotional beings—we also learn that there are appropriate and less-appropriate ways to act in response to these feelings. Understanding our emotions and the way we respond to people and incidents is a significant part of human development.

Social Development

This learning of restraint and self-control is one aspect of social development. Human beings are social creatures and learning how to interact appropriately with others is another key part of development. The domain of social development is wide-ranging, and at least somewhat culturally informed. Mastering a culture's expectations of appropriate behavior, eye contact, physical contact, gender norms, work habits, and more are all part of social development. Social development also involves things like organizing groups, navigating conflict, and collaborating with others. Students come to school having already been socialized in family structures and are further socialized through their experiences at school. Educators seeking to foster their students' social development can often do this best in partnership with others.

Spiritual Development

One last developmental domain we should consider is spiritual development. This developmental domain is often a bit slipperier than the others. The old saying goes that faith is more often "caught" than "taught." In a discussion about spiritual development in young adolescents, my friend, Syd Hielema, once quipped, "Faith formation is sort of like trying to nail Jell-O to the wall."[43] What he meant is that it can be tough to pin down just how spiritual development takes place in kids. But at the same time, there are models that can be used to describe students' spiritual development,[44] and tools that can be used to document faith formation.[45] For Christian educators in particular, consideration of how young people move from knowing the facts of Bible stories, to understanding the faith lessons being taught through those stories, to understanding the big themes and truths of Scripture, to their own profession of faith can help us to guide the young people entrusted to our care and foster their spiritual formation.

Each of these developmental domains are important, and this is not an exhaustive list of all the ways kids are developing and changing as they grow and mature. Teachers need to know patterns of development, and what typical kids at the grade levels they teach are like. Understanding these patterns can help us ensure that our teaching is developmentally appropriate for the kids we are serving.

Teaching Whole People

When we start looking at all these developmental domains, it can feel a little overwhelming. Human beings are complex! Perhaps it's no wonder then that many teachers begin to focus just on cognitive development, which seems most closely in line with the academic focus of our work. But as thoughtful Christian educators seeking to teach Christianly, we need to broaden our focus. Our students are whole people, created in the image of God himself.

I love the story in Mark 12 where Jesus is being tested by the Teachers of the Law. One of them asks him the question, "Of all the commandments, which is the most important?" Jesus's response reveals so much about how he views human beings, and I think there is a lesson for us as teachers in this as well. To this expert in the law, who knew all the Old Testament laws inside out, Jesus says this:

> The most important one is this: 'Hear, O Israel: The Lord our God, the Lord is one. Love the Lord your God with all your heart and with all your soul and with all your mind and with all your strength.' The second is this: 'Love your neighbor as yourself.' There is no commandment greater than these.[46]

With this teaching, Jesus is calling us back to the heart of the Law, and why God gave his people the law in the first place: as guidance for living in right relationships with our God and our fellow human beings. But this teaching reveals something essential about how we are created to be as well.

In his unpacking of this passage, Andy Crouch suggests that this passage lays out a "compact summary of what being fully human involves."[47] Crouch's definition for what it means to be human is based on Jesus's teaching from Mark 12 about the greatest commandment: "Every human person is a heart-soul-mind-strength complex designed for love." He continues on, saying,

> A human person is not a mind without a heart. You are not a brain without a body. You are not a body without a soul, nor were you ever meant to be a soul without a body. You are all of these, together, and it is this complex of qualities that makes you a person. Each of us is a combination of several parts that add up to something more.[48]

What Crouch is getting at here is an essential idea: human beings are complex! While it sometimes makes sense for us to focus on just one aspect of our integral selves, we must remember that we are whole beings, more than just the sum of these parts.

To be specific about it, teachers have to watch out for overemphasizing just the "mind" aspect—students' cognitive development. Schools surely are academic institutions, and we do have a primary emphasis on learning, which often prioritizes the mind. And there may be times when it is *right* for us to focus just on students' minds, or their cognitive development. But I think we must be cautious about this, not forgetting that our students are more than *just* their minds. We human beings are much more than "brains-on-a-stick" as James K. A. Smith puts it.[49] This does not mean that we should not focus on learning, obviously! But we must recognize that our students are whole people.

Jesus surely loves the little children, and he loves every part of them: heart, soul, mind, and strength. And we too, as God's children, are called to love him, and to love our neighbors with our whole selves: heart, soul, mind, and strength. We were designed for love, and perhaps this is one of the finest ways we too can reflect God's image: God is love, and his image-bearers are called to love with every part of ourselves. We love because he first loved us![50]

Questions for Reflection after Reading:

1. Think of a younger child you know; did this discussion of developmental domains make sense to you in light of what you have observed in this child? Why or why not?
2. What is a new idea that helped expand your imagination?
3. What challenged your thinking, or what question would you like answered?

Chapter 8

Jesus Loves ALL the Little Children
Learner Diversity

Taylor's Journal . . .

I walked in on an unsettling conversation in the teachers' workroom today. Jake was complaining—loudly—about a student by name. He was saying such terrible things about this kid's poor work habits and how he was such a negative influence on his classmates. And then, the worst part: Denise chimed in with, "Oh, I know just what you mean—he was in my class last year, and I couldn't wait for the year to be over. He is the worst student I've ever taught. Sorry you got stuck with him this year, Jake. I bet you've already started your end-of-the-year countdown!"

Now, I understand that we sometimes need to share the burden about our struggles with students, and colleagues probably understand better than anyone else what we're going through as teachers. But I felt horrible that two of my colleagues were having this kind of grinch-fest about a student in a semi-public place. What if that student had walked by in the hall just then? I was so disappointed in this, and now

I'm feeling a little guilty that I didn't speak up and say something!

Predictable Patterns . . . and the Unpredictability of Diversity

In the previous chapter we briefly touched on the idea of patterns of development that are present in every age group of students. There definitely are patterns we can discern and knowing patterns of what is typical for an age group is so valuable as a teacher. Understanding our students' capacities—physically, cognitively, emotionally—can help us right-size our teaching to ensure that it is appropriately challenging without overwhelming students.

While it is certainly true that we can see these patterns, we also must recognize the joyful challenge of unpredictability when working with human beings. Our students are not machines, or little robots that we can program and ensure they will behave in exactly the same way. Equal inputs do not ensure equal outputs with real, complex human beings!

Think of it this way: while we can describe what a "typical student" is like in terms of patterns of development . . . our students are all unique individuals. Even in a classroom group of 20, or 25, or 30 students, few will truly fit exactly into that "typical student" mold. What is a typical kindergartner? A typical grade 3 student? A typical middle schooler? A typical senior in high school? When we are labeling a student as "typical," we are actually comparing them to the norm of the pattern of development for their age group. We are sort of saying, "Here is what an average kid is like." But the reality is that few students are "typical" when we consider them individually.

I was a middle school teacher for many years, and I had a seventh-grade homeroom for almost all of those years. I loved teaching young adolescents! There is *so much* development that happens between the ages of ten and fifteen, and there is perhaps more diversity present in a group of seventh graders than at any other point in their school career. Think of all those developmental domains we discussed previously: students are growing and changing physically, and cognitively, and socially, and emotionally, and even spiritually through their middle school years. And this development is not smooth and even! Picture a group of seventh graders and you might begin to see what I mean. Some kids develop physically earlier than their peers, but their emotional development lags behind. Some kids' cognitive development is way ahead of their classmates, while their emotional maturity is slower to unfold. There are "men" in boys' bodies, and "boys" in mens' bodies, and they are all out on the basketball court together. There are young ladies whose physical development is catching the eyes of older boys, and who do not yet have the social and emotional development to deal with the attention they are receiving. Some kids seem overly emotional, while others have learned to coolly handle challenges with grace and calm. Some are asking incredibly deep questions about faith and the nature of reality, while others never seem to wonder anything at all. All these diverse kids are "typical" 13-year-olds! They are growing and changing at different rates—different from each other, and even as individuals their development in different domains can seem out of sync. None of them are "average." Each one is a unique individual, with strengths, weaknesses, gifts, talents, and challenges of their own.

We need to consider that two things can be true at the same time: we *can* describe patterns of development . . . and we can *also* realize that individual kids will not always fit those patterns. Diversity of individuals means that the predictable patterns simply don't always hold true, because real human beings are more complex than a statistical analysis might predict.

We Teach the Students We Have

One important thing that you need to keep in mind as an educator: rarely do you get to choose your students. Rather, we teach the students assigned to us. We have a professional responsibility to teach the kids—to teach *all* the kids—that are on our class list.

Remember the three loves we discussed in an earlier chapter? Great teachers love *who* they teach, *what* they teach, and *how* to teach. I think that loving kids is the ticket for entry to this profession; if you don't love your students, you simply should not be a teacher. That said . . . I wonder sometimes if there is a difference between loving students and liking them. I always love my students, even when they are difficult and teaching them feels more like a burden than a blessing. But in my heart of hearts, well, there are times I am not sure I like some students. Or at the very least, I don't like what they do. Can we love students we don't like?

Here is one of the real challenges of teaching Christianly: we must love our students—all our students! But more than that, I think we must continue to grow and develop in *liking* our students as well. In my experience, kids can tell when you don't like them. It comes through in subtle ways: a micro-expression that flashes across my face, the way I phrase a response, the kind of feedback I write in response to a student's homework, my body language when interacting with them. All of these can reveal things about how I feel about my students in miniscule ways that might not seem important. But the accumulation of these small things can give students the impression that they are not liked. And if they are not liked . . . they might begin to feel that they are not loved.

So perhaps this is one of the joyful challenges of developing a teacher imagination: how can you convey to students that you do like them, even if you don't always like the things they do? Can you separate their actions and your responses to those actions from their personhood? This is not at all easy, but it's a shift we must begin to make. Shifting from a feeling that "I have to" work with challenging students to a mindset of "I *get* to" work with challenging students might be a first step.

Sometimes it's the chemistry of the group that makes it challenging. I have had this situation several times over my teaching career. When engaging with students as individuals, I can almost always find likable things in every single kid, things to celebrate, things that bring me joy, gifts and talents I can name for each one. But somehow, as soon as the mass of the class comes together, there is something in the alchemy of the whole that shifts these delightful individuals into a collective monster that is perplexing to manage. Here again, approaching the management of the group with an "I get to" instead of an "I have to" might be the first step. Untangling complex interpersonal knots takes time and effort, but it is a key part of our calling as Christian educators: to be peacemakers, to be community-builders, to be ambassadors of reconciliation.

It might seem that it would be easier to teach students if they are all the same. Honestly, this might be true, and there have been days that I've wished for a little less diversity among my students, just because it might make things a bit easier for me. But the reality is, diversity is a *good thing*, and it's the way God has created us human beings. God surely must love variety; just standing on the edge of a prairie-full of wildflowers, or tide pool bursting with sea life, or a classroom of diverse learners all created in God's own image is enough to see his delight in his varied creative works. God did not intend human beings to all be identical, as if we were little robots to be programmed and commanded. But this certainly does not mean that meeting the needs of a diverse group of students is an easy task. And diversity appears among a group of students in a multitude of ways.

How Does Diversity Show Up in Schools? (Let Me Count the Ways . . .)

What immediately comes to mind for you when you hear the question, "How does diversity show up in schools?" Perhaps you first think of racial and ethnic diversity? That is a common response, and an important one. But there are many other ways that diversity appears in any group of students: varying socioeconomic status, different home and family situations, various languages, a range of abilities and disabilities, and many different intelligences are all part of the rich mixture of a diverse classroom. Let's briefly consider each of these to help expand our imaginations of how diversity impacts teaching and learning.

A diversity of races and ethnicities in the classroom is a beautiful, joyful thing—perhaps a glimpse of the throne room of heaven the Apostle John describes in Revelation:

> After this I looked, and there before me was a great multitude that no one could count, from every nation, tribe, people, and language, standing before the throne and before the Lamb. They were wearing white robes and were holding palm branches in their hands. And they cried out in a loud voice:
>
> > "Salvation belongs to our God,
> > who sits on the throne,
> > and to the Lamb."[51]

While I absolutely love this picture of unity—with people of every background standing together in worship—we also must recognize that on this side of Christ's second coming, this is generally *not* the way things look today. There is often much strife between people of different races and ethnicities. Part of developing our imagination as teachers is developing a sense of cultural competence so that we can work to bridge gaps. This takes humility; I only know the skin I walk around in, and it is incredibly presumptuous for me to act as though I understand the experiences of people from different racial and ethnic backgrounds than the one I have experienced firsthand. This means we have to position ourselves as learners. We must be curious, willing to listen, willing to engage. Making our classrooms a space that is hospitable for people from all sorts of racial and ethnic backgrounds will take work, and a willingness to keep learning.

Similarly, we should carefully consider the variety of socioeconomic backgrounds that will likely be present among the students in our classrooms. Some families have more wealth and tangible resources than others, and poverty is a real problem, and not just when it comes to schools. That said, poverty does have an impact on students' learning. Decades of social science research demonstrate a correlation between socioeconomic status and academic achievement in school.[52] The reasons for this correlation are debatable and have been debated hotly for some time. But few reputable scholars of education would argue with the premise that children coming from a lower socioeconomic status have the deck stacked against them in some ways, while students from wealthier families have advantages. None of this is fair, and we should grieve the situation. An awareness of this disparity is the first step in working to address it.

Language is another source of diversity we should consider. Depending on the place you live, there is likely a majority language, or even an official language.[53] Regardless of any "official" language status, most schools have students who are language learners, who do not (yet) have mastery of the majority language. This can provide huge challenges for learning—and for teaching too. Most language learners will need encouragement and targeted support to succeed as they are working to learn the majority language in addition to learning everything else in the curriculum!

Students come to school with an array of diverse abilities and disabilities. In the typical classroom today, you are likely to find students with a range of learning disabilities, such as dyslexia (a disorder affecting reading and language-based processing), dysgraphia (a disorder affecting writing and fine-motor skills), dyscalculia (a disorder affecting understanding of numbers and learning math facts), auditory processing disorder (a disorder affecting distinguishing between sounds). Students with a variety of mild to moderate physical and cognitive disabilities such as visual impairment, hearing impairment, speech and language impairment, and intellectual disabilities are also present in typical classrooms. Students with ADHD, autism, and various mental health concerns from depression, to anxiety, to obsessive-compulsive disorder, to bipolar disorder are all likely to be part of the typical class group today. Some students are identified as "gifted and talented," meaning that they have one or more areas in which they have the capacity to perform at significantly higher levels than their typical peers.

All these students will likely need some modifications to the "typical" lesson plan for them to learn, succeed, and flourish.

One more area of diversity we should consider is the variety of different types of intelligence that students exhibit. Intelligence was once viewed as something you had or did not have, a singular trait that could be quantified by a test.[54] While some psychologists still view intelligence as a general, singular trait that you have more of or less of, many researchers and scholars have shifted to thinking of intelligence as a collection of different abilities, or different ways of being "smart." Gardner's Multiple Intelligence Theory is a very popular one, that suggests eight different ways that intelligence manifests:

- Linguistic intelligence—being smart with words, reading, and writing
- Logical-mathematical intelligence—being smart with numbers and logical reasoning
- Spatial intelligence—being smart with how you perceive space, like navigating with a map, or packing a suitcase efficiently
- Bodily-kinesthetic intelligence—being smart with how you use your body, like dancing, playing soccer, or juggling
- Musical intelligence—being smart with rhythm, making music, and even enjoying music
- Naturalist intelligence—being smart with seeing and documenting patterns in nature
- Interpersonal intelligence—being smart with understanding other people and interacting with them
- Intrapersonal intelligence—being smart about yourself, your own beliefs, and your personal capabilities

The idea of Gardner's theory is that every person has each of these different intelligences to varying degrees, and that we can generally develop our capacities in each of these areas to at least some degree. (Though we should recognize that there are likely some limits to our abilities to do this. I can develop my bodily-kinesthetic intelligence by practicing free throws and left-handed layups on the basketball court . . . but I am never going to play in the NBA!)

Another example of a theory that explains intelligence as a variety of areas is Sternberg's Triarchic Theory of Intelligence. As the name suggests, this theory explains that there are three main ways that intelligence is manifest:

- Creative intelligence—the abilities to develop novel, resourceful solutions to problems
- Analytical intelligence—what we might call "book smarts," the abilities to think logically and rationally to solve problems
- Practical intelligence—what we might call "street smarts," the abilities to apply common sense to solve problems

One thing I really like about Sternberg's theory is that he focuses on developing wisdom, and he argues that wisdom comes from using all three of these forms of intelligence. And when you think about kids you know, perhaps you can readily see one or more of these three intelligences more readily in them? That is an opportunity to capitalize on a strength that they have.

Thinking through different ways that intelligence manifests in individuals can give us opportunities to make the curriculum come to life for each student. We can perhaps see that some students have more depth in some areas of intelligence while they also have room to grow in other areas. Recognizing the variety of intelligence strengths our students bring with them into our classrooms can help us teach them in ways that bring about their flourishing as human beings.

Clearly, there are lots of ways that diversity manifests in a group of students! The joyful work we have as teachers is ensuring that *all* the students ensured to our care and instruction are learning. To do this effectively means we have to get to know our students as unique individuals, because each has his or her own story. Learning about each child takes time and dedication, but it's a tangible way for us to live out the expectation that teachers both love and like their students.

Seeing Students through Jesus's Eyes

In a previous chapter we were considering what a biblical anthropology looks like. As human beings, our students are both created good, and also totally affected by sin. This means that we have to simultaneously look for the good, and also recognize that they will sometimes—perhaps often—fall short of what we might hope for them in terms of their behavior. This concurrent beautiful-and-broken nature of students can drive a teacher a little crazy! There are days when they are amazing, delightful human beings, and teaching them feels like the most thrilling work I can imagine. And . . . there are also days when their sinful human nature rears its collective ugly head, and teaching them is the hardest, most heart-breaking work I can picture, and I wonder why I would continue to subject myself to this kind of pain. In those hard days, it's essential to keep in mind a third part of a biblical anthropology: Jesus loves the little children.

Learning to love the kids—*all* of the kids—is a never-ending journey on this side of glory. This is an essential aspect of teaching Christianly, I think: we need to see our students through Jesus's eyes. They are innately lovable, not because of anything they have done, but because they are created in God's image. Yes, they are sinful. And because of this, they need care, discipline, correction, and instruction. Jesus loves them; he loves them enough to literally die for them. Thanks be to God that the redeeming work is done—we cannot save our students!—but out of joyful service to the Lord, we have the privilege of working to build his kingdom day-by-day in our classrooms. Loving our students, and *liking* our students, is part of that work.

Part of seeing our students through Jesus's eyes is being careful not to label students. This is challenging! As we see all these ways that diversity shows up in students, it might be tempting to label them as "the student with OCD," or "the ADHD kids," or "the Spanish-speakers," or "the kids from single-parent homes," or even "that difficult kid." I must resist the temptation to make one of these ways that might illustrate a child's uniqueness into their defining feature in my mind. Recognizing that each kid is a whole person helps move past the labels that we might attach to them. This, in turn, can help us see them as lovable, broken-but-beautiful image-bearers.

Meeting the needs of a diverse group of learners is *hard work*, and we should not pretend otherwise! When we start to see all the diversity present within a group and find that the chemistry of the class makes teaching them a challenge, we might feel overwhelmed. The good news: we do not do this work alone. The Holy Spirit is working in us and through us. I believe that God blesses our efforts, feeble as they might be some days. He can do amazing things even in our weakness! Perhaps the most important question for serving students to the best of our ability is, how willing are you to engage with them as the unique individuals that they are? Are you willing to get to know your students?

Questions for Reflection after Reading:

1. Think about your own school experiences; does the discussion of different ways diversity manifests in groups of students make sense to you? Why or why not?
2. What is a new idea that helped expand your imagination?
3. What challenged your thinking, or what question would you like answered?

Chapter 9

Culture and Climate

Creating a Space Where Learning Can Happen

Taylor's Journal . . .

I found a note on my desk this morning, clearly left there by a student. It was just three sentences:

> School is hard for me, but I love being in your class.
> You never make me feel dumb for not understanding things.
> You are the best teacher I've ever had.

It wasn't signed, but I am pretty sure it was from Sara. She sure does struggle with her schoolwork. But what gem she is! It breaks my heart a little to think about her comment about being made to feel dumb—who has done that to her in the past? Classmates? A family member? Maybe even a teacher? (Ugh . . . I hate to think that!)

This year I've really been putting a lot of effort into creating a classroom climate where everyone can flourish. I've been wondering if it's actually making a difference at all, but this note is a good indication that it is making a difference for Sara at least. And if it makes a difference for even one kid, well, then I think it's worth all the effort!

Do Students Have to Like Their Teachers to Learn from Them?

Picture your favorite teacher. Can you imagine yourself back into their classroom? What did it look like? Sound like? Feel like? What was your impression as a student being part of that class? Most of us have at least one teacher that holds a special spot in our memories, due to the positive impact they made in our lives.

Now picture your *least* favorite teacher. Imagine yourself back into their classroom. Does it look different? Sound different? Feel different? Unfortunately, most of us have at least one teacher that looms large in our imaginations as a relatively negative influence in our lives. I wish this weren't the case! But sadly, it seems to be almost universal.

And now . . . think about a class you took at some point in your school career that seems hard to even remember. Maybe there is a subject that you know you must have studied at some point, but you can hardly recall anything from that class. Not that it was such a negative thing . . . but it also wasn't a positive thing in your life? No highlights or lowlights, just a blah, beige experience? What might this mean? Who was the teacher leading that class anyway?

Most people will say that they like some teachers more than others; this is quite normal. But can you learn from a teacher you don't like? I am not convinced that the teacher being liked is a prerequisite for students learning in that class. In fact, I know I learned a lot from several of my teachers who I may not have always liked—because they were so strict and had such high expectations for our learning. But I also know that for me, as the teacher, I would much prefer that my students like me than that they don't like me. I think where some teachers run into trouble is that they are focused more on the *liking* than on the *learning*. Learning is the goal, and our professional responsibility is to ensure that students will learn! But I also think that the conditions for learning matter greatly. And when I think about all the teachers I've had throughout my life, the best teachers were the ones who created an environment centered around *learning*. As a side effect, these classrooms also tended to be the classrooms where I liked the teacher . . . and I was sure that the teacher loved me.

Here is the terrifying truth about our work: the teacher is the essential variable for creating a classroom environment where learning happens.[55] I sort of wish this weren't the case because it feels quite daunting to imagine that we have this kind of power! But conversations with students over decades of my professional life as an educator suggests this is true: the teacher is *almost always* the deciding factor in whether a classroom is a place the students feel is welcoming and joyful, or stressful and awful, or nondescript and boring.

Those called to teach should grapple with the influence we hold, for good or ill, over our students' experience in our classrooms. Remember when we discussed the teacher's "office" in a previous chapter, we focused on the nature of power in the classroom. I think we must carefully consider how we use the power of our office when it comes to the classroom environment. We can use that power in ways that bless students, or in ways that students perceive as a curse. How can we develop a classroom atmosphere that blesses our students and invites them into flourishing?

What's the Weather Like Today?

I was a science teacher for many years, and I find that continue to draw teaching metaphors from nature. Let's take a brief side trip into a science lesson, shall we?

There is a blanket of air surrounding planet Earth. Air is a complex mixture of gases: over 75 percent nitrogen, nearly 20 percent oxygen, about 1 percent argon, just under 0.5 percent carbon dioxide, and many more small fractions of other gases, including water vapor. This layer is frightfully thin, compared to the size of the planet; if the Earth was the size of an apple, the atmosphere is about as thick as the peel of the apple. But that thin layer of gases surrounding our planet is absolutely vital for life to exist on this planet! Obviously, we need the oxygen in the air, as it plays an essential role in all sorts of chemical reactions both inside our bodies and out. But there is more to the atmosphere than just breathability. The blanket of air surrounding our planet provides protection from many small meteors that burn up and vaporize as they blaze towards us. Our atmosphere helps shield us from harmful ultraviolet radiation from space. The air around us transmits sound waves, so we can hear things—with no air, our sense of hearing would be dramatically impeded. Additionally, our atmosphere is an important part of keeping the Earth a habitable place: it helps to insulate our planet and regulate temperatures, so days aren't too warm to endure, and nights aren't too cold to survive.

This last fact about temperature regulation is the key for understanding weather. Weather has to do with the temperature, humidity, and air pressure in a particular area. As masses of air warm up and cool down we can see dramatic changes happening in the weather. Winds are moving masses of air, from gentle breezes, to kite-hoisting gusts, to umbrella-flipping gales, to tornados. Clouds of all shapes and sizes illustrate movement of water vapor through the atmosphere, and the different kinds of precipitation we see are all results: rain, snow, hail, sleet, and thunderstorms. Huge movements of wind and water, like hurricanes and typhoons can result from the accumulation of many small changes in local weather. In other words, weather is the evidence of local atmospheric conditions.

Over time, we can see patterns emerge in the local weather conditions. These patterns we call "climate." The climate of a region can be described as the "normal" weather conditions over time. For example, I currently teach in the upper Midwest, and people sometimes joke, "If you don't like the weather, just wait an hour, because it will change." We expect hot, humid summers where thunderstorms are likely. We expect autumns that slide from warm September days through crisp Octobers into chilly Novembers. We expect winters full of bracing winds whipping across the prairies, punctuated with snow and ice and an occasional blizzard. We expect springs to be a slow, muddy thaw, with rain likely throughout the warming up to summer.

In contrast, when I taught in southern California, we expected hot, dry summers, and less hot (and less dry) winters, and mild spring and fall that would ease us between these seasons. Snowstorms were unheard of. Even thunderstorms were rare; we had *one* thunderstorm in a three-year period! I could almost always tell what the weather would be just by looking out the window in the morning. If it was winter and the sun was shining, it would probably be about 68 degrees Fahrenheit (about 19 Celsius) for the high temperature with little chance for rain—I would grab a light jacket and head out the door. I think that being a meteorologist in San Diego must be about the most boring job in the world! This is because the climate there is just so . . . consistent . . . there are few surprises.

Now, why this detour into an Earth science lesson? I think that contemplating weather and climate can be a very helpful way for us to understand what is happening in a classroom. Classrooms too have an "atmosphere." And just as the oxygen in Earth's atmosphere ensures our survival, the atmosphere of the classroom is vital for learning to flourish. The classroom atmosphere can vary from day to day, just like the weather. And, over time, we can see patterns develop, and thus we can describe the climate of the classroom as well.

So how does the daily weather arrive? What creates the classroom climate? Here, again, is the terrifying truth that we educators must grapple with: the teacher is the driving force of almost every part of the classroom atmosphere. The renowned educational psychologist, Haim Ginott, said something very similar to this in his book, *Teacher and Child*, where he wrote:

> I have come to a frightening conclusion. I am the decisive element in the classroom. It is my personal approach that creates the climate. It is my daily mood that makes the weather. As a teacher I possess tremendous power to make a child's life miserable or joyous. I can be a tool of torture or an instrument of inspiration. I can humiliate or humor, hurt or heal. In all situations, it is my response that decides whether a crisis will be escalated or de-escalated, and a child humanized or de-humanized.[56]

The idea in this quote resonates with me deeply, and I have found it to be true in my own experience as an educator. My choices, my plans, the way I respond in the moment . . . all of these determine whether students will experience sunshine, or frost, or thunderstorms in my classroom today. Certainly not every day will be warm sunshine; we teachers are human, after all. But neither should every day be a howling blizzard!

Further, when we consider the type of climate we are striving towards, it's helpful to think in terms of the average over time. What is the *general* pattern in the classroom atmosphere? Are the conditions generally warm, with gentle showers and light breezes? If most days for the teacher are hailstorms or hurricanes, this is a real problem. But we should recognize that we teachers are whole people, and there will be stormy days on occasion. Bearing in mind that these kinds of weather events are usually not the norm, we can foster an atmosphere where learning—and learners themselves—can flourish.

Hospitality, Belonging, Engagement, and Joy

If we think about the kind of classroom where learning—and learners—will flourish, there are several key elements to the atmosphere that teachers should consider. What will make the classroom a space that will draw students in with a magnetic pull, a place they will *want* to be? A place where deep learning will be the norm? There are four pillars I see for creating this kind of classroom atmosphere: hospitality, belonging, engagement, and joy.

The first characteristic of a classroom atmosphere where learning flourishes is hospitality. Hospitality carries with it a connotation of *welcoming*. The word "hospitality" comes from a Latin root, *hospes*, meaning "host." If we are hospitable to our students, we are welcoming them in, making a space ready for them to be cared for. Perhaps it's no wonder that the words "hotel" and "hospital" share the same root—these are places where people are hosted and cared for as well. I want to suggest that what the space *looks like* is less important than what it *feels like*, if we are aiming for true hospitality. I once heard a sermon that contrasted "hospitality" with "entertaining," and that always stuck with me. When we are entertaining, we are putting on a show. When we are being hospitable, we are welcoming. A hospitable classroom is one where everyone is welcome to come as they are. But hospitality is not the end, it is merely the beginning of creating a classroom where learning will flourish.

A second characteristic of a flourishing classroom atmosphere is belonging. Students must certainly be welcomed in, but what are they welcomed into? They are welcomed into a community of belonging. Think about what it means to belong to a group. If you truly *belong*, you are a member, you are needed. To be a needed member means, "we are less than without you here." I am drawn to the imagery Paul uses in I Corinthians 12 of the Body of Christ, where he says, "The eye cannot say to the hand, 'I don't need you!' And the head cannot say to the feet, 'I don't need you!'"[57] Every member of your body is needed, and every member has an essential function. Likewise, in a classroom where learning flourishes, every student must experience that same kind of belonging. God created us to thrive in community, and this means we must also learn in community. Teachers who are intent on fostering this kind of classroom atmosphere should consider the role of both competition and collaboration in their classroom—and which of these results in the kind of space where *every* student belongs.

A third atmospheric characteristic to consider is engagement. When students are truly engaged in learning, they cannot be apathetic; learning is the opposite of boredom! Engagement carries a connotation of activity; when students are truly learning they cannot be passive. Teachers looking to create an atmosphere of engaged learning should thoughtfully consider not just what they are teaching, but also *how* they are teaching. The content should be meaningful and accessible to students . . . but the *way* students engage with that content matters. This does not mean there is not a time and a place for "just telling them;" lectures can be a very effective and efficient way to convey some content to students. But experiences are almost always more engaging, interactive, and memorable. Teachers must consider using teaching methods that will capture students' attention and imagination: stories, demonstrations, research projects, hands-on experiences, fieldwork, debates, experiments, design projects, and discussions are almost always more memorable and more formative learning experiences for students. These kinds of learning experiences are almost always going to be challenging, high-interest, and interactive—just the sorts that are going to promote lively engagement. Injecting a little mystery, creativity, inquiry, or personal investment from the students is almost always a sure bet to make for a more engaged atmosphere for learning.

Finally, teachers seeking to create an atmosphere where learning can flourish should consider the role of joy in their classroom. Is your classroom ruled by joy, or by fear? I suspect that joy and fear cannot truly coexist. A joy-filled classroom is one marked by celebrations—celebrations of the gifts of individuals and the community, celebrations of achievements, celebrations of learning. Joy is not the same thing as happiness. I think of happiness as situational, and more fleeting. Joy is abiding, and long term. Joy is a way of life that we get to pursue.[58] Joy manifests through gratitude, delight, playfulness, hopefulness, and optimism. Joy does not mean that every day needs to be a party in the classroom, but rather that we should practice revelry—looking for opportunities to be merry, to laugh, to see and celebrate the good. The Christian life is not easy, but it is joyful. Similarly, a classroom in which the teacher is striving towards teaching Christianly will almost certainly be an illustration of a joyful spirit.

Hospitality. Belonging. Engagement. Joy. Just imagine how a classroom marked by these characteristics would feel for students! This is the kind of classroom atmosphere we should strive for: welcoming and caring, member-oriented and communal, active and interactive, delightful and celebrative. The climate of this kind of classroom surely will result in flourishing of learning, because the learners themselves will be flourishing.

Building a Pedagogical Home for Your Students

Reading this chapter, a cynic might say, "Well all this stuff about the learning environment is fine and good, but what about the *real* work of teaching?" That's a fair question to ask, I think. Some folks want to get right down to the business of planning lessons, and choosing teaching methods, and devising assessment strategies—these aspects of the profession that feel like the central aspects of teaching. And please hear this right: planning, instruction, and assessment *are* essential parts of the work teachers do. But I want to emphasize that fostering this kind of learning environment is *also* the real work of teaching. All the planning, instruction, and assessment are carried out in the context of a learning environment, and we must consider where the teaching and learning will be taking place.

What we're really talking about here is *pedagogy*. The word "pedagogy" comes from two Greek words: *paidos*, which means "child," and *agogos*, which means "leader." So "pedagogy" is literally "leading children," which is truly what teaching is all about, isn't it? Guiding young people on the journey from not knowing to knowing? From not understanding to understanding? This is why we have already spent so much time in thinking about how kids grow and develop, and how diversity manifests in a group of students: without understanding development and diversity, it's hard to lead them well!

A helpful way of thinking about pedagogy is to consider it as "the art and science of teaching." Pedagogy is a science in the sense that we can use research-based strategies that are more effective for ensuring that students will learn. But pedagogy is also an art in the sense that each teacher has their own unique approach in the classroom in which they put those teaching methods into practice. John Van Dyk captures this idea of teaching as both an art and a science by calling pedagogy a "craft," suggesting that the craft of Christian teaching involves "both technical know-how and personal intuition."[59]

Good pedagogy then involves both an understanding of both the nuts-and-bolts of the "science" of good teaching *as well as* the "artistry" of the individual teacher capitalizing on their own strengths, gifts, passions, talents, and personality to breathe life into those methods. Your pedagogy is where *you* show up as the teacher. Your teacher imagination is on display as you conduct your craft; your pedagogy is the embodiment of your beliefs, your thinking, your heart, your creativity. Your identity and integrity as teacher are most obviously evident in your pedagogy.

This is why all this focus on the learning environment is so crucial: the teacher has a responsibility to craft an atmosphere where learning can happen. Remember, the teacher is the essential variable for creating a classroom environment where learning happens! And this means that the way you imagine your role in creating that learning environment really matters, teacher.

It's easy for us to get lost in the methods of teaching, and to perhaps over-emphasize the techniques teachers use. We certainly *should* consider our methods, of course. But the work of teaching is much more than just our techniques. I appreciate David Smith's take on this idea. Smith says,

> We should step away from seeing teaching as a set of techniques, as something done *to* students by a teacher. When we teach, when we design learning, we offer a temporary home in which students will live for a while, and we shape the patterns of life together within which they will grow. A pedagogy is a home in which teachers and students can live together for a while, a place to which students are welcomed as guests and in which they can grow.[60]

Devising a classroom-home where students and teachers alike can learn, and grow, and thrive is central to the work for educators devoted to teaching Christianly. The kind of learning environment we craft absolutely matters for the way we live out our faith in our teaching!

Questions for Reflection after Reading

1. Does the metaphor of the classroom as a pedagogical home that exhibits hospitality, belonging, engagement, and joy resonate with you? Why or why not?
2. What is a new idea that helped expand your imagination?
3. What challenged your thinking, or what question would you like answered?

Chapter 10

Knowledge and Understanding
What Do You Need to Know to Be a Teacher?

Taylor's Journal . . .

I got Charlie today, which had me feeling great. Oh, that kid drives me crazy sometimes with his shenanigans, but what a smart cookie he is! He reads everything, and the insane thing is that he remembers every detail of every book he has read. And he loves to try and stump me, and he often does. But not today!

Out of the blue today, he asked me, "Do you know what an anablep is?" And I replied, "Yep! They are four-eyed fish that like to sit right at the surface of the water with two eyes looking at what's happening above the surface, and two eyes watching what's happening under the water. They are such weird, wonderful creatures." Charlie's eyes bugged out and his mouth dropped open. "How did you know that??" I just grinned at him and said, "I have my ways."

Little did he know, I ran into his dad this morning before school, and he told me that Charlie was planning to ask me what an anablep is in class today. Apparently, Charlie often tells his dad what he's going to try and stump me with *each day—that stinker! That kid is going to win big on a game show someday with that headful of trivia he's got. Thankfully, I don't have to be a quiz-game master to be a teacher, but it's interesting how teaching has helped cement an awful lot of facts into my mind too.*

Loving, and Knowing, and the Challenges of the English Language

There are some ways that English fails as a language. I'm cautious saying this, because I am one of those people who is truly fluent in only one language, and it happens to be English. But there are some shortcomings to the English language, and in particular the lack of nuance we have in some situations.

Consider the word "love" as an example. I use the word "love" in lots of different contexts. For example, I love to read . . . and I love chocolate chip cookie dough ice cream . . . and I love my students. I love my wife. I love my kids. I love my dog. I love superhero movies. I love listening to folk-pop and nineties alternative rock music. I love building model rockets. I love Jesus.

Are all of these loves the same? Certainly not! The way I love ice cream and the way I love Jesus are *not at all* the same! The way I love some music genres and the way I love my students are *very different*. Even the way I love my kids and the way I love my dog are similar in some ways, but loving people is still different than loving animals. Loving people, versus loving things, versus loving activities, versus loving the Creator and Sustainer of all things . . . they aren't the same, right? What I'm suggesting here is there is nuance in the way these "loves" are made manifest in my life. And yet, I use one word to describe my relationship to each of these people and things: love.

There is a similar problem with the word "know." Are there different kinds of knowing? I think so. Often, we might think of knowledge as something we *have* or *do not have*, a singular quality of whether we've captured and filed away a piece of data. For example, do you know how far the earth is from the sun? Do you know when Henry VIII died? Do you know where Ouagadougou is located on the map? Do you know who wrote the 1812 Overture? Do you know the chemical formula for glucose? These are all things you could look up and "know." But is just having a mastery of facts enough?

Similar to the way "love" is nuanced, I think there is more nuance in thinking about "knowing" as well. There is a difference between knowing a person and knowing *about* a person, for example. There is also a difference between knowing facts and having a deeper understanding of why those facts matter. Being able to win a trivia game demands one kind of knowing, but that might actually be the shallow end of the pool when it comes to depth of knowledge.

Considering that idea of depth of knowledge, let's get more specific. What does it mean if we would say that a student "knows multiplication?" We might mean that the student has memorized the basic facts of multiplication, that they know 2 x 1 = 2, 2 x 2 = 4, 2 x 3 = 6, etc. If they have memorized their times tables, do they "know multiplication?" We might also mean that they have learned an algorithm for solving multiplication problems, so when they see a problem like, "What is 239 x 317?" they have a plan of attack for how to calculate the answer. Or . . . we might mean that they have a deep number sense and knowledge of mathematical operations, that they genuinely understand how multiplication works and *why* it works that way, and maybe that they could explain it to someone else, or perhaps that they can apply their understanding to new situations that they have never encountered before. In each of these cases we might say a student "knows multiplication." But to what depth do they know it? Is it just rote memorization? Or a basic understanding? Or a deeper ability to apply, and analyze, and explain?

What does it really mean to know something? A further question: what do teachers need to know to do their work? And, perhaps most importantly, to what degree to we need to know things to teach others?

Different Kinds of Knowing—Content, Pedagogy, Development, and More

Teachers need to have a mastery of multiple domains of knowledge to teach effectively. These knowledge domains overlap a bit, but that just points to the complexity of the work of teaching, and why we need to develop a teacher imagination!

We could start with knowledge of practical skills. All teachers need to have effective communication skills, such as the ability to read and write fluently, and a level of comfort speaking in front of a group. At least a foundational mathematical knowledge is necessary for all teachers. Basic technology skills have become important knowledge for teachers as more digital tools continue to become part of classrooms today. Understanding of a school system and the teacher's place in it is important knowledge, as well as the responsibilities of different members of the faculty and staff. While different schools may have their own unique policies and procedures, things like where to get resources, how to request purchases, when to take your students to lunch, where to line up for transportation at the end of the school day, and other "small" details of running the school day are all practical things teachers need to know, and things that are relatively easy to learn once you become a member of the faculty in a school.

While these practical areas of teacher knowledge are certainly important, these are probably not the areas that need some expanding teacher imagination. There are larger domains we must consider. For example, teachers need to have content knowledge: they need to know the material they are going to be teaching to their students. For example, if you are a music teacher, you need to know how to read music, and understand harmony, and rhythm, and know a bit about music history and probably a wide variety of songs, and perhaps how to play one or more instruments. Or if you are a math teacher, you need to know problem solving strategies, and number sense, and algorithms for calculating, and at least a bit from algebra, and geometry, and statistics, and probability. Or if you are an art teacher, you need to know color theory, and design principles, and perspective and space, and a wide variety of techniques for making different kinds of art, and probably at least a little art history. The big idea here is that different content areas have different areas of focus, and so teachers who are working to help students understand that content must know the content themselves!

Another essential knowledge domain for all teachers is pedagogical knowledge. Pedagogy is "the art and science of teaching." So pedagogical knowledge is knowledge about how to teach—and knowing that there are a wide variety of different methods we can use as we teach. Pedagogical knowledge involves knowing how to set appropriate learning targets for students, and how to ensure that our lessons will be designed to support students meeting standards. Planning out an appropriate sequence of activities to ensure students learn is an underrated skill; it's hard work, but something great teachers do effectively as they continue to develop their pedagogical knowledge. Pedagogical knowledge also includes assessment strategies and knowing what kinds of assessments will be the most effective for confirming students' knowledge, understanding, and skills. Writing a good test, developing an engaging project, creating a useful rubric to guide the evaluation . . . all of these are part of a teacher's pedagogical knowledge toolbox. And let's not forget the teaching methods! Perhaps this is what comes to mind first when we think about pedagogy: how can I best ensure students will master the content? Should I lecture? Should I use a demonstration? Should I assign something to read? Should I show a video? Should students do research to answer their own questions? Should we use collaborative learning? Knowing how to use these different kinds of strategies—and many more!—are all part of a teacher's pedagogical knowledge base.

We should not forget the things we discussed in earlier chapters about knowing about students in terms of both their development and uniqueness. Student knowledge is another essential teacher knowledge domain. Understanding the developmental characteristics of the students at the grade level you are teaching is critical for ensuring that your instruction is developmentally appropriate. This means you can—and should—tailor your teaching of the content to your students' developmental capabilities. We want to stretch students as they learn . . . but we can't teach content that is too far out of reach for them, or they won't learn it. Likewise, if we are teaching content that students have already mastered, they aren't really learning, right? There is a time and place for reinforcing knowledge, of course, but if we want students to learn new skills and help them develop deeper understanding of the content, we need to keep in mind their development. Likewise, remembering the many ways that diversity shows up in a group of students can help you to ensure that your instruction will meet the needs of the variety of students you get to teach. Knowledge of students helps you apply your content knowledge and pedagogical knowledge effectively.

In fact, this brings up another knowledge domain we should briefly consider. If we imagine content knowledge and pedagogical knowledge as overlapping circles, we could picture a Venn diagram like this:

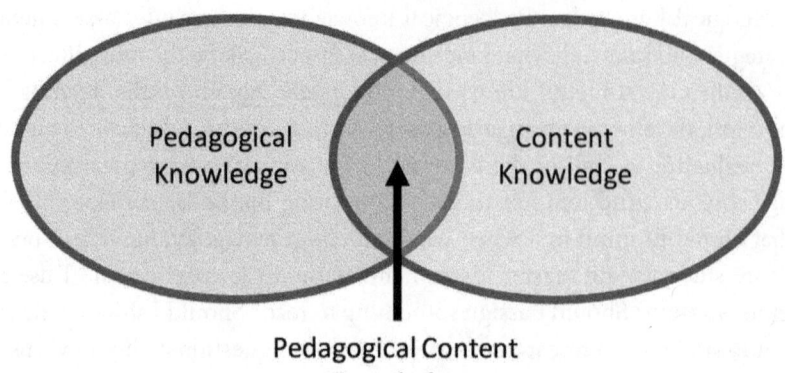

The overlap between pedagogical knowledge and content knowledge could be considered "pedagogical content knowledge," as Lee Shulman named it in the 1980s.[61] Pedagogical content knowledge goes beyond just knowing the content to understanding how different approaches to *teaching* the content will influence students' understanding of the content. Does that idea make your head spin a little?

The big idea of the pedagogical content knowledge domain is this: teachers use different pedagogical moves depending on the content we teach. Shulman described pedagogical content knowledge as being comprised of "the most regularly taught topics in one's subject area, the most useful forms of representation of those ideas, the most powerful analogies, illustrations, examples, explanations, and demonstrations—in a word, the ways of representing and formulating the subject that make it comprehensible to others."[62] Another way of saying this: teaching music is different than teaching math, which is different than teaching art, because the *content* being taught is different, and so we must use different teaching methods. Further adding to the complexity of this is ensuring that we are putting our pedagogical content knowledge to work considering our knowledge of our students, as this also impacts and influences our approach to the content and our pedagogical decision-making. Whew! There certainly is a lot we need to know to be effective teachers.

How Much Content Knowledge Is "Enough" to Teach?

One question I grappled with early in my career as a teacher was, "Will I know enough about the content I need to teach?" To be fair, I am old

Knowledge and Understanding

enough that the World Wide Web was still a bit of a novelty when I began teaching. I grew up in the era before Google. Today we might have an opposite, but related, question: "Will I know enough that my students don't fact-check me and demonstrate that I have gaps in my content knowledge?"

At the heart of each of these concerns is the wondering of how much content knowledge is "enough" for teachers. And, like so many questions in the field of education, the answer is likely, "It depends." The depth and breadth of content knowledge you need depends on the grade level you teach, and the number of different subjects you teach.

At the elementary level, teachers are much more likely to teach many subjects—perhaps even *all* the subjects!—their students will pursue. This means a broad content knowledge is extremely valuable for teachers at these grade levels. Elementary teachers should have at least *some* knowledge about reading, writing, spelling, grammar, mathematics, science, history, geography, civics, art, music, and health, and the list could probably go on and on! Do all elementary teachers need the same depth of knowledge in all these areas? Perhaps not. But a broad knowledge will best equip them for the wide variety of subjects they are likely to teach.

At the middle school level, teachers generally focus more closely on fewer subjects. This was my own experience as a middle school teacher: I often taught only one or two subjects (math and science, in my case) which meant I could develop deeper knowledge of just a couple of subjects. At the same time, the nature of middle schoolers and their diverse curiosity meant knowing at least a little about many other subject areas was very helpful, not least of which when I was helping students in a study hall with their literature homework, or practicing maps skills, or reviewing for a history test. While depth in a couple of content areas is obviously valuable, having some breadth in content knowledge is still very beneficial for middle school teachers.

By high school, many teachers focus in just one discipline. For example, math teachers need a deep understanding of mathematics because the demands of the content at the secondary level are much deeper: to teach trigonometry, a math teacher needs a robust understanding of both algebra and geometry. Likewise, high school English teachers are likely to teach a variety of literature, writing, and grammar courses, which means they need deep understanding and experience with the English language. It is less likely that high school teachers will teach a variety of different subjects, so a deeper background in just one subject (or perhaps two closely related subjects, such as history and government) is traded for the breadth that is more common in younger grades.

And then there are teachers who teach multiple grade levels! This is most common in some specific content areas, such as music, art, and physical education. In these content areas, teachers need to develop deep understanding of their content, and the way they employ pedagogical content knowledge will be deeply influenced by their knowledge of the students—they will definitely need to adapt the content for the developmental level and diversity within each group of students.

Special education teachers perhaps are a category of their own when it comes to the content knowledge they need. Teachers in special education are likely to work with students at a variety of grade levels, and in a variety of content areas, no matter the grade level at which they teach. So, a breadth of content knowledge will certainly serve them well. But particulars of the needs of the unique students they serve mean they may leverage a different set of pedagogical skills and apply their pedagogical knowledge very particularly in light of their knowledge of students. How much content knowledge do they need? Perhaps this is still the key question that is ringing for all teachers, not just special educators.

The good news for all teachers is that we can—and must!—continue to develop mastery of the content we teach throughout our careers. There is a natural expansion of human knowledge over time. We continue to learn more about this world God has made, and as our collective understanding grows, there is always more for us to learn, and in turn to teach our students. Knowing "enough" content to get started and being willing to keep on learning is one mark of a great teacher.

Knowledge and Your Teacher Imagination

The drive to want to know things is a normal part of being human. Most people have an innate curiosity, a desire to know things and understand how things work. This is true of young kids, for sure; any pre-school teacher can tell you how many questions kids ask! This carries through elementary school as well; kids' natural curiosity is relatively easy to capture, and we can use this to drive their learning. And while we might sometimes think that middle schoolers, and high schoolers, and even adults aren't as curious as young kids, I wonder if there is some social pressure to not appear too eager to learn. Maybe this is a behavior or attitude we pick up along the way? That it isn't cool to want to be curious? I wonder this, because in my experience, when given the opportunity to learn things that are personally meaningful to us, most of us are still curious, and will use that curiosity to keep learning.

I think this desire to learn, and wonder, and understand is part of how God created us to be. Much of the Wisdom Literature in Scripture—Job, Psalms, Proverbs, Ecclesiastes—point to knowledge, understanding, and wisdom. Considering a bit of the wisdom from these books might help expand your teacher imagination around what it means to know things, and what it means for us to help students know things as well.

For instance, Psalm 19 might be one of my favorites as a former science teacher. It begins with these words:

> The heavens declare the glory of God;
> the skies proclaim the work of his hands.
> Day after day they pour forth speech;
> night after night they reveal knowledge.[63]

Creation itself speaks God's glory! And the more we learn about how God has created this world, the more we can wonder and worship. Verses like these remind me of the joyful work we get to do as teachers: we have the opportunity to stand in awe of our Creator, and to guide our students into those same moments of wonder and worship.

Another passage that might be a little less well known, but also informative for our work as educators is found in Proverbs 25:

> It is the glory of God to conceal a matter;
> to search out a matter is the glory of kings.[64]

I love this verse, because it reminds me that God has created us to be curious, to search things out, to seek understanding. God is the creator and sustainer of all things, and he can conceal things at his pleasure. But he has created us human beings with a desire to know, to learn, to discern. Solomon, who is traditionally named as the author of Proverbs, is renowned for his wisdom.[65] In 1 Kings 4, Solomon is described as knowing all about plants and animals, so perhaps Solomon was describing his own learning and curiosity in saying that searching things out is "the glory of kings?" Regardless, this is a good reminder for Christian teachers and their students alike: our curiosity and capacity to search things out is part of how God created us.

That said, I also believe there are limits to human knowledge and understanding. The book of Job illustrates this truth very well. Job's story is fascinating, and one I do not have time or space here to tell fully; you should just read the whole book for yourself! But to recap, the book of Job is a story of the problem of suffering, where we find Job, the righteous friend of God tested by all sorts of trouble. Job's friends argue that bad things don't happen to good people, so Job must have some secret sin that is unconfessed, and that is why God is afflicting him. Job maintains his righteousness—and we as the readers are able to see behind the scenes that God is allowing Satan to test Job's faith. Near the end of the book, Job finally says something along the lines of, "God, I've had enough of this, and I feel like I deserve some answers." And the most terrifying thing happens: God does answer Job![66] The Lord's answer to Job is four chapters of questions that illustrate that God's awesome power and wisdom are so much greater than our own—God does not owe us any explanation—and yet, God loves us, and cares for us, and reveals himself to us. And finally, Job sees his sin: self-righteousness, and a sense that he is entitled to understanding God's ways. Job's response to God's questions is so illuminating:

> I know that you can do all things;
>   no purpose of yours can be thwarted.
> You asked, 'Who is this that obscures my plans without knowledge?'
>
>   Surely I spoke of things I did not understand,
>   things too wonderful for me to know.
>
> You said, 'Listen now, and I will speak;
>   I will question you,
>   and you shall answer me.'
> My ears had heard of you
>   but now my eyes have seen you.
> Therefore I despise myself
>   and repent in dust and ashes.[67]

I take this response to mean that Job "gets it": he has had an encounter that reveals who God really is, and how much bigger God's knowledge is than human knowledge. This too is a good reminder for us as educators: we simply cannot know everything. As much as we learn, there is always more to learn. And there are some things we will never understand, hard as that might be for us to accept. Perhaps we too need to have an encounter with the Omnipotent Creator to better understand the limitations of our own understanding!

What I'm trying to suggest here is that there are limits to the depth of our knowledge and understanding. We are finite beings, limited in our mortality. But this does not mean that God does not invite us to wonder, to inquire, to learn. To reiterate, I believe we are created to want to know and understand. So what guides our quest for knowledge? Perhaps it's no wonder that a favorite verse of many Christian educators is Prov 1:7, which says

> The fear of the Lord is the beginning of knowledge,
> but fools despise wisdom and instruction.[68]

This reminds me that curiosity is something to celebrate, and that growing in understanding is a blessing. This proverb encourages us to remember that increases in knowledge and understanding grows out of learning to love the Lord—the root of real wisdom.

Perhaps that is where we should wrap up our thinking on this topic for now. What is growth in knowledge and understanding *for*? What is the intended goal of knowing, after all? Is it so we can pat ourselves on the back and celebrate just how smart we are? Or is it aimed at something bigger, something better? True wisdom, I think, is seeing that our knowledge will never be complete, no matter how hard we study or how much we learn. And yet, God invites us and expects us to grow in wisdom, and to guide our students in the paths of wisdom. What an awesome invitation that is!

Questions for Reflection after Reading

1. What knowledge domains do you need to learn more about to become a more effective teacher? Why?
2. What is a new idea that helped expand your imagination?
3. What challenged your thinking, or what question would you like answered?

Chapter 11

Finding the Path
Curriculum Guides the Learning

Taylor's Journal . . .

Everyone at the staff meeting this morning was buzzing—we heard that the legislature might be mandating some curriculum changes. It seemed like everyone had an opinion about it, with some people thinking it was about time, and others thinking this probably spells the end of education as we know it. I know I haven't been teaching that long, but it seems to me that curriculum resources are often changing. Deb, who was sitting next to me, leaned over and basically said the same thing: "Well, it's probably about time for a new textbook anyway, right? I guess there are upsides and downsides to changing curricula." But then Jake turned around and muttered to both of us, "Well, they can change it if they want to, but it's not like we're all just going to follow along with whatever they say, right? I mean, it's not like those politicians are going to be hanging out in my classroom checking in on me."

I have been thinking about that comment all day. I understand where Jake is coming from, for sure. But I feel like I *have a professional responsibility to teach the curriculum I'm given. How much choice do I really have in the way I implement the content I have to teach?*

A Little Language Lesson: What is "Curriculum" Anyway?

I suspect you've heard the word "curriculum" before, but you might not have ever considered what it means. Some people equate curriculum to a teacher's manual or a student textbook. Others picture lengthy documents that list all the standards to be taught and the benchmarks for student learning. Still others might think of curriculum as something more active, such as writing lesson plans, or listing learning targets on the board for students, or plotting out learning activities. Still others might picture document designed as a list of topics to be covered or a guide to assessment. It's understandable why any of these concepts might come to mind when we hear "curriculum"—each of them captures part of the story. But I think a little language lesson might be helpful for understanding what curriculum is actually all about.

When I was in middle school, I had the opportunity to take a variety of electives that extended my learning in light of my personal interests. I took ceramics, and model rocketry, and journalism, and photography—all things I enjoyed deeply as a young adolescent. One other elective I took that has ended up being very useful throughout my life: Introductory Latin. While I only had one semester of Latin, it helped me immensely when I was studying Spanish in high school, and it even helped me better understand English, since there are plenty of English words and grammatical structures that have Latin roots.

Take the Latin word for "to run" for example: *currere*. If you know a Romance language (that is, one based on Latin), you'll probably recognize this word. In French, "to run" is *courir*, and in Spanish, *correr*. But even in English you'll find derivatives of the Latin *currere* all over the place when you start looking for it. Consider the word "current," which is the flow of a "running" stream, or electricity "running" through a wire. Or think of the word "course," which is the path we follow when running a footrace. "Occur" also is related: the thought that "runs" through my mind in a moment is something that "occurs" to me. The words "corridor" and "excursion" and "discourse" all share this root as well, and all of them have that sense of movement built into them. And—as I suspect you may have guessed by now—the English word "curriculum" also shares its linguistic root with the Latin *currere*. At a literal level, the "curriculum" is the path we follow through the content of a course.

Perhaps an analogy will help you to imagine curriculum this way. Picture yourself standing on the edge of a field that stretches out in front of you. The field represents a subject area: maybe this field is science? Maybe it is art? For the purposes of this illustration, let's imagine the field is mathematics. Now the content of this field is "mathematics," but there are many possible paths we could take through this field. One path might be named "algebra," and there are certain topics that we would find on that path. Another path might be named "geometry," and this route would go in a different direction through the field than the "algebra" path. Other paths through this field would include "statistics," and "trigonometry," and "calculus." Some of these paths travel in parallel to each other, while many take their own wandering routes through the field. Can you picture it?

Each of these paths through mathematics illustrates a *course*, a path to follow through the field. And how to do we know if we are on course? A map would certainly help, right? And that is perhaps a helpful way to think of curriculum. Curriculum is the map of the path we are taking through the content of a particular field.

To enrich this picture, think of the content of an algebra course. There are particular "stops" along this path, including "variables and expressions," "functions," "linear equations," "quadratic equations," "systems of equations," "factoring polynomials," and the like. There are some places where this path runs in parallel to the path we call "geometry"—places like graphing, and exploring parabolas and circles and ellipses. But knowing what should be on this path helps us stay on track and not get distracted by all of the other possible topics in the field of mathematics: our focus in this course is algebra. From the path we call "algebra" we might see intersections with other paths, like trigonometry and calculus, but those aren't the point of the path we are following. The curriculum of this course has a specific scope (what is included and excluded) and sequence (the order in which we come to the topics). This is how following a path works in real life, after all: we can usually tell when we're going off course (out of the scope) and we have to cover the first mile before we can go on to the second mile (sticking to the sequence).

Finding the Path

I find this metaphor of the curriculum as a trail we are hiking helpful for imagining what curriculum truly is: the curriculum we teach is a path through the content that students will learn. It's also helpful for helping us imagine our role as teachers: we are guides on the path.[69] If you've ever been hiking on a demanding trail, you know the benefit of an experienced guide. Your guide knows the path ahead and can help you stay on course. Your guide can help you avoid possible pitfalls. And your guide can point out must-see vistas to ensure you don't miss the best parts! Guiding our students through the curriculum is the essential way that we *apply* our content knowledge and pedagogical knowledge and put it into action through our work as teachers.

Using Your Resources: Textbooks and Teachers' Guides

At the beginning of this chapter, I mentioned two ways people often picture "curriculum": either a stack of textbooks, or a list of curriculum standards. I hope that the alternative picture I've been painting of the metaphor of the curriculum as a path to travel is challenging these kinds of mental pictures for you, but let's explore each of them briefly, and why they don't hold up as useful depictions of what curriculum really is.

For many people—even professional educators—if you would ask them about the curriculum of a school, they would probably start by describing the textbooks that are a ubiquitous part of school today. When you hear "textbook" you might be picturing a big book dedicated to a particular subject, like a literature anthology of short stories and poems, or a book full of math exercises. Or perhaps you're picturing a digital textbook that you access through a web browser, with built-in interactive elements? Whatever the format, textbooks have a long history in formal education, stretching back to at least 300 BC, with Euclid's *Elements* which is regarded as the first Geometry textbook.[70] And there are certainly Chinese, and Egyptian, and Babylonian writings that go back much further than that!

Right along with the student textbook you might be picturing the teachers' guide that goes along with the text. Teachers' guides are useful tools, usually including the student text with margin notes for teachers giving suggestions for how to teach the material, including questions to ask the class, answer keys for student exercises, and further background and context for the content of the lesson. Many teachers' guides also include a variety of other resources that teachers can use to enhance and supplement the textbook. These additional resources might be useful for assessing student learning, reteaching concepts students haven't yet learned, and providing additional ideas for enrichment and extension beyond the textbook itself.

Textbooks and teachers' guides are useful tools for teachers! They lay out a scope and sequence to the content to be learned. They can provide structure to the learning, and to the teaching as well. They give support to busy teachers who might be planning multiple lessons in multiple subjects every day. But all of that said, the textbook is not the curriculum. Textbooks and teachers' guides are valuable *tools* that teachers can use to develop and enact the curriculum.

If the curriculum is that path we are taking through the content, a competent teacher will plot out the path they are guiding students down with care. A teacher's guide can be helpful for mapping out that path. It can provide a reasonable scope and sequence for the learning, and the readings and exercises in a student textbook can be valuable supports for learning the content. But the danger for teachers who begin to see the textbook as their curriculum is that the become a slave to the textbook. That is, they stop thinking for themselves about what students need, and just keep marching through the content regardless of students' interest. Sadly, some teachers become such slaves to "covering" the content that they begin to focus much more on their teaching than on student learning. In this mindset, the teacher says, "Well, I taught it . . . I covered the content . . . it's not my fault if the students didn't learn it!" I am pointing the finger at myself as I say this, because I know I've been this teacher at some points in my career. But the problem I see is this: if the students didn't *learn* the content . . . did you really teach it? Simply covering the material in the content isn't enough!

Please hear me right: I am *not* saying that teachers should not use textbooks and teachers' guides. Particularly at the beginning of your career as a teacher, you will almost certainly find these to be very useful tools! But they are just tools, and the tools are not the curriculum. So, we must wisely consider how we can *use* these tools to help us guide our students along the path to understanding as we explore the content. And we should also consider what other tools we should draw in that will help ensure students will understand the curriculum. Books, online resources, video clips, podcasts, guest speakers, field trips, and more can all be used as curriculum resources as you plan a path through the content.

Learning Targets and Curriculum Standards

Now we might find ourselves at another problem, however. If you have a mountain of possible content sources, how do you determine which ones you should use? Maybe your teachers' guide is a helpful place to begin your planning, but then you find another book you want students to read, and a guest speaker on the topic, and an excellent field trip in your area that could really enhance students' understanding, and then there's that online game you found . . . and suddenly you're spending three weeks teaching a lesson that might only need two days to ensure students understand the key concepts!

It's easy to lose focus with so much content to teach, and so many resources to bring in to support students in learning that content. How can we regain focus? This is where learning targets can be very helpful. We will talk more about learning targets in a future chapter that is all about planning, but for now, let's just say that learning targets help you keep your focus—your aim—on the crucial knowledge, understanding, and skills that all students must learn. Knowing what we are aiming for can help us to judge which resources we should utilize.

How do we set learning targets? This is where your multiple knowledge bases come together. Knowing your students is key, both their developmental levels as well as the things that make your unique group of students their unique selves. Your pedagogical knowledge also comes into play here: knowing a variety of teaching strategies can help you to write a more effective learning target, because we use different strategies in different content areas. Teaching a literature lesson is different than teaching a lesson in physical education, and having a clear sense of what you will do—and what you will have students do—as they learn the content helps you stay on target. Knowing the structure of the discipline you are teaching is helpful: where does this lesson fit within everything students will be learning in their history class this year? Where does it fit with what they will be learning throughout the social studies curriculum in your school? That kind of content knowledge is important for ensuring that we are keeping on target.

But how will we know if the target we are aiming for is on the path to understanding that we are seeking to guide students along? This is where curriculum standards can be very useful.

Curriculum standards are short statements that articulate what students should learn at a particular grade level. Standards documents have been created by various professional education organizations. For example, in the United States, the National Council of Teachers of Mathematics (NCTM) has published a set of standards that they believe all students should achieve in their math education throughout grades K-12. These standards are broken down by year, so you can look up what students in grade 4, or grade 8, or any other grade level should be learning, according to NCTM. Other professional organizations such as the National Council of Teachers of English (NCTE), the American Association for the Advancement of Science (AAAS), the Society of Health and Physical Educators (SHAPE), National Council for the Social Studies (NCSS), and many others have developed content standards for their areas of focus. Each of these standards documents lay out the professional consensus of what content should be taught at each grade level within these content areas.

Standards documents like these can be very useful for teachers and schools as they map out their curricula for different content areas! Knowing what the experts in these disciplines recommend is a useful way to check the curriculum to ensure it meets expectations for what students ought to have the opportunity to learn at each grade level. Teachers can use these standards to write learning targets that help them keep focus on the key knowledge and skills that students should learn as they encounter the content.

That said, standards are not the curriculum. The path we plan through the content can—and should—be informed by standards. But in our metaphor of guiding students along the trail, curriculum standards might best be thought of as way-markers along the path. We might think of them as checkpoints to ensure that we aren't wandering too far off the path as we guide students. The challenge is including the right number of way-markers on the path; when hiking, you don't need a way marker every three steps on the trail! Similarly, it's possible to try and cram in too many standards, which takes away the teacher's creativity, and probably a fair bit of their passion as well. So while standards are valuable and can provide support and guidance for a teacher in planning the curriculum, the standards themselves are not the curriculum to be enacted.

Imagining the "Real" Curriculum

Planning and enacting curriculum is one of the most creative parts of a teacher's craft, and this is another spot where the work of imagination comes into play. In an earlier chapter I suggested that the work of imagination in teaching involves both playfulness and practice. I think that curriculum is a place where these two aspects come together meaningfully.

Recall our metaphor of curriculum as the path we are guiding students down towards understanding. The whole idea of "guiding" suggests that there is a sort of direction-setting in this aspect of teaching.[71] If we are guiding students down a path, it implies that we have mapped out where we expect them to go . . . and ideally, it is a path we've traveled ourselves! But the first time you teach something, it might feel a little uncertain. This is where using those teaching resources and curriculum standards can be especially helpful for mapping things out—as well as the expertise of experienced colleagues who may have traveled this path before! But the best way to be equipped to guide students is to get out there and follow the path yourself. Your content knowledge is important, and you'll be applying it as you develop the curriculum you are leading students along.

But here's the conundrum: the only way to become a veteran teacher with ten years of experience . . . is to go out and teach for ten years, right? So, a word of encouragement: plan well for the first trip down the path with your students, but do this playfully, and with a plan that you are going to keep practicing and learning from what you practice. This might sound scary, because on your first time through the content you are tasked with teaching you might not be 100 percent sure of where you are headed, but trust that your playful planning will be enough to prepare for this trek. I hope this liberates you a bit from the worry that your students won't learn; they certainly will learn—and you will learn things too, just through the joy of teaching them and traveling the path with them!

The truth is, I've had many opportunities to teach new things throughout my career, and I have reached a point where I think the old adage that "the third time's the charm" is true. The first time I teach something, it's exciting, and a little terrifying, and so I plan fastidiously. But I also have taught long enough now that I realize that some things that are not going to go as I have planned them, *and that is okay*. Students will still learn, even as I am learning to teach this new thing! There will be some things that I will say, "Well, I know I won't do it that way again next time!" but that is part of the playfulness I'm talking about—recognize that your first time down the path with students will probably not be exactly the way you'll travel the path the next time around, and that is good, and normal!

The second time I get to teach the new thing, it always seems to go a little better, a little more smoothly. The things I learned the first time down the path inform my next trip. Sometimes this means fixing the broken pieces I discovered the first time through. Sometimes this mean playfully trying a different approach, or a different resource, or reworking the sequence of activities a bit. The second time down the path is still a learning experience—for the students, and for me as well. But I find my certainty as a guide growing: I'm better able to point out the "can't miss" vistas and nudge them away from pitfalls along the way. Practice instills confidence.

And then, the joy of the third time I get to teach the new thing! The third time down the path, I know so much more of where I'm headed through this content, and the curriculum path feels much more secure and surefooted. This doesn't mean I'm on autopilot; a good guide is always watching, always mindful, always on the lookout for the good of those being led down the path. And so it is for teachers: continuing to play and practice with the curriculum we teach will continue to build our confidence, but the point of this is ensuring our students will learn. Our nudging them along the way is part of the refining process of our mastery of the curriculum.

And after the third time we lead students down this curriculum path? Have we arrived? Certainly not! On this side of glory, we will never "arrive." We can continue to learn, to grow, to improve, to align our practices more closely with the way of Jesus. This is the "real" curriculum, the real path we ourselves are following, after all. Imagining the curriculum paths we will use to guide our students through the content is important work. But as Christ-followers, we too are on a path laid out before us.

The writer of Hebrews puts it this way: "let us throw off everything that hinders and the sin that so easily entangles. And let us run with perseverance the race marked out for us, fixing our eyes on Jesus, the pioneer and perfecter of faith."[72] The course, the path—the "curriculum," if you will—is already marked out for us. And this idea of Jesus as the pioneer—the trailblazer—captures my imagination and inspires me! We can trust and rely on the Lord to guide us on this path, not just through the content we teach, but through our whole lives. And this is one of the ways we reflect the model of Christ in our work as teachers: teaching Christianly means proclaiming "Jesus is Lord" throughout work, whether in what we say or what we do. The way we approach applying our content knowledge and planning curriculum is a demonstration of our faith a very tangible way.

Questions for Reflection after Reading

1. Does the mental picture of curriculum as a path through the content help you better understand the concept of curriculum? Why or why not?
2. What is a new idea that helped expand your imagination?
3. What challenged your thinking, or what question would you like answered?

Chapter 12

Designs for Learning

Planning and Preparation for Effective Instruction

Taylor's Journal . . .

I discovered something this week: I *really* like writing lesson plans. It's funny for me to realize this because I did *not* always love writing lesson plans in my college classes. I remember complaining to one of my professors about the format we had to use: "Come on . . . NO professional teacher would write this kind of detailed lesson plans every day—it's way too much work!" My professor's answer then seemed a little hollow to me: "You're right, professional teachers don't write plans using this format. But . . . you're not a professional teacher yet." She smiled at me as she said this, and I know it was meant kindly. But it took me a few years of teaching to realize the truth of that statement. Learning to plan effective lessons was a little like learning to ride a bicycle: I needed training wheels at first—the structure of that lesson plan template we had to use.

But my realization this week was that my planning practices have gotten a lot more efficient as I've gained experience. That first year, I basically wrote a script for every lesson I taught, which was exhausting! But now, I have activities planned out that I can just adjust a little as needed, and slide decks ready to go, and discussion questions I've tested and tweaked. I guess the way I'm thinking about planning today is so much more about the *learning my students will be doing*, instead of the *teaching that I am doing*—and that is making all the difference!

The "Real" Work of Teaching: Planning, Assessment, and Instruction

As we've explored a teaching imagination, we've covered quite a bit of ground. We started by thinking about teacher identity, calling, and how our faith motivates our work as Christian teachers. We considered a bit of the history of education and some of the contemporary challenges of the profession. We explored professionalism and ethics, and leadership, and office-consciousness. We pondered learner development, and learner diversity, and how we can begin to create learning environments where all our students can learn and grow. We investigated the different knowledge domains teachers need, and how we can apply this knowledge as we develop curriculum. I hope that all these considerations have helped to expand your imagination of what teaching Christianly looks like in each of these different aspects of the teaching profession.

But by this point you might be thinking, "All of this is well and good, but what about the 'real' work of teaching? How do we actually *teach*?" That's a fair wondering! I hope that you can see how all these topics play in the background, but we also should think about the actual work of teaching. With this chapter, we're going to take a turn to consider the three main aspects of teaching: planning, assessment, and instruction. In this chapter, we'll focus on planning, which is one of the most important things teachers do. In the next two chapters, we'll zoom in on assessing student learning, and then consider the various instructional methods and strategies we use. You will see that these three aspects are all interrelated, but it may help to talk about them separately to get a clearer sense of what is involved in each one. So, let's dive in and start by thinking about planning.

"Fail to Plan . . . Plan to Fail?"

There is an old saying that "if you fail to plan, you should plan to fail." While that might sound dismal, there is an element of truth here. There are times when the busyness of teaching means we must make hard decisions about how we will spend the limited time we have. But neglecting planning will almost certainly result in sub-par teaching . . . and sub-par learning for students. It's true that some teachers can wing it from time to time and still find some success, but it's a rare teacher indeed who can shoot from the hip and hit the target every time. The truth is, planning takes time and effort, but it's time and effort well spent!

Planning is the place where we take what we know about our students, what we know about the curriculum, and what we know about good teaching, and carefully construct a design for learning. Planning is fundamentally about design: designing opportunities for students to come to deep learning. Without making time to plan carefully, teachers typically veer into one of two equally problematic approaches to teaching: activity-focused teaching, or coverage-focused teaching.[73]

Activity-focused teaching errs on the side of having students be very busy *doing* lots of things without clear purpose. These activities can be fun for students, and are often organized around a theme, and may involve engaging projects. But such activities and projects may or may not be carefully aligned to learning targets that ensure deep understanding of concepts. We can rightly wonder whether students are focused on the right things in the whirlwind of activities. Will the activities students are doing really result in meaningful mastery of the key knowledge, understanding, skills, attitudes, and beliefs?

Coverage-focused teaching, on the other hand, errs on the side of marching through the textbook without regard to students' interest, actual curriculum priorities, or even real learning. In an age of long lists of content standards and overstuffed textbooks, it's no wonder that some teachers trend towards simply "covering" the content. But when thinking about this coverage approach, we should wonder whether students truly have the opportunity to play around with ideas, to investigate, to ruminate, to reflect . . . to *learn*. Wiggins and McTighe suggest this approach might just as well be called, "Teach, test, and hope for the best!"[74]

Making time to plan with care can help avoid veering into either of these problematic approaches. As Harro Van Brummelen puts it, "Meaningful learning in the classroom does not come about by chance. It presupposed careful planning. Educators do not achieve meaningful learning by simply following a textbook or by providing interesting learning activities."[75] Designing effective instruction demands a teacher imagination, and the intentionality of both a little playfulness and deliberate practice—with the payoff of deeper learning on the part of students. But this is hard work, and we shouldn't pretend otherwise! Planning lessons that will keep your students engaged in meaningful work that is both relevant to their lives and accessible to them is demanding.[76]

One of the real challenges for teachers, particularly early in their careers is to flip from thinking more about the *learning* than about the *teaching*. Frankly, it's easy for teachers to get caught up on the things we will be doing as we teach, and not think enough about the things students will be doing as they learn. While we certainly must be aware of our moves as teachers, we should *first* ask, "What will the students do to achieve deep learning?" and then consider the teaching moves we will need to use to make that deep learning a reality.[77]

I recognize that I'm really leaning hard on the importance of strong planning here. You might then be wondering, "Okay . . . but isn't there ever a place for some freedom and spontaneity in teaching? Just letting things happen and unfold as they will? Won't kids learn that way too?" These are good questions to ask! I do not mean to suggest that we never have unplanned flashes of delight in the classroom, or that there is no room for serendipity in teaching. There really is such a thing as the "teachable moment," when a student asks the perfect question that is worth pursuing, even if it isn't on the lesson plan for the day, or when world events and students' lives come together in a way that letting go of the plan for the day is the right thing to do. We *should* make use of those magical moments and take advantage of them. But the reality is that careful planning allows for us to be able to make these kinds of pivots on the fly when teachable moments arise. Without intentional planning, students' experience in the classroom is likely to be disconnected, jumbled, and haphazard, and the learning that occurs will almost certainly be shallow and random.

I hope my point is becoming clear: it is always possible that learning will just "happen" spontaneously in some moments in the classroom. But if we take seriously our responsibility as teachers, we will plan carefully to ensure student learning. The word *ensure* is a scary word! But that is our professional responsibility as teachers. If students aren't learning, are we really teaching?

My argument is this: if we are serious about ensuring learning, we must thoughtfully and intentionally make design decisions that will ensure students' learning. We can do this by carefully selecting high-engagement learning activities without sliding into the activity-focused orientation, and by mindfully using our resources to stay on course through the curriculum without careening into the coverage-focused orientation. But to do this effectively, we will also need to think about the different scales of planning.

Scale of Planning: Yearly Plans, Unit Plans, Lesson Plans, Daily Plans

When you hear the phrase "planning for instruction," where does your mind go? Do you picture a teacher preparing materials for tomorrow's class meeting? Do you picture a teacher with a calendar in hand, mapping out where they will be in the textbook by Christmas break? Do you picture a teacher sketching out the day, moving from one subject to the next? All of these are aspects of planning, because planning happens at different scales. It's helpful for us to think about planning as a way of structuring and sequencing learning. Our designs have different levels of detail at different scales.

Yearly Plans

Almost every novice teacher knows the feeling of coming to the last month of the school year and finding that you still have far more than a month's worth of content left to teach. What do you do then? Go into fast-forward lecture mode and try to teach 30 pages of the textbook every day? Pick and choose a few favorite topics to highlight? Decide to just teach one well-crafted unit, and scrap the rest of the curriculum for the year? Throw up your hands and cry? Perhaps it's no wonder that some teachers drift into the coverage orientation: there is so much content to teach, how can we do it all?

Laying out a tentative-but-realistic plan for the year can help avoid this situation. A yearly plan gives you the broad strokes of the curriculum and how you intend to implement it. In your yearly planning, you'll be setting realistic goals for yourself and for your students. You might think of it month-by-month, saying, "By October 1, we should be this far, by November 1 we should be up to this, and by Christmas we should be wrapping up with this project." Your school might have a pacing guide that suggests a week-by-week (or even day-by-day) breakdown of the content to be taught. These kinds of guides have some benefits, especially for teachers new to the profession. Their potential downside is that it is easy to start just marching through the curriculum to the drumbeat of the pacing guide without considering what students really need. Remember that our students are real human beings, not robots for us to program and expect them to all behave in precisely the same way. Some flexibility in your pacing will almost certainly be needed. But that is the idea of yearly plans: they are intended to help keep us on track over the course of the whole year so we can more effectively respond to students' needs and ensure their learning.

Unit Plans

The curriculum you teach will likely be made up of some segments that are arranged topically, or thematically, or conceptually. These segments are often called "units." For example, a middle school pre-algebra curriculum might typically include units on factors and multiples, ratios and proportions, fractions and decimals, percentages, variables and expressions, and solving equations. A high school biology curriculum might typically include units on cellular functions, genetics and heredity, diversity of living things, and ecosystems. An elementary art curriculum might typically include units on color, shape and line, drawing, sculpture, and famous artists.

The units in a curriculum are arranged in a particular sequence depending on the needs of the students, or the structure of the discipline. Sometimes students need to master one part of the curriculum before they will be able to understand the next unit, as is often the case in mathematics or science courses. Other times, the curriculum is arranged chronologically, as in a history course, or thematically, as is more common in a literature course. As we plan units, we should keep in mind the broader structure of the course, thinking about what came before this unit, and where we are headed next, so students can get a sense of the flow of the curriculum as well.

What defines the structure of a unit? Units are typically designed to ensure students meet one or more broad learning goals. Goals for different subject areas will look different but are typically focused on the big ideas that students should have the opportunity to learn. For example, when I was a middle school science teacher, I taught a unit on chemical reactions.

Student goals for this unit included, "I can explain chemical and physical properties that can be used to identify different substances," and "I can describe several ways to identify a chemical reaction." You can perhaps already imagine some learning activities I would include to help ensure students can meet these goals—things they should read, demonstrations they should have the opportunity to observe, investigations they should conduct firsthand, and research they should do to deepen their understanding. This is the main idea of unit goals: the learning activities students do in the unit should all trace back to the goals so we can ensure students will master the big ideas.

In the same way, unit-level assessments should be aimed at these goals and should be carefully constructed to ensure they measure students' achievement of the goals of the unit. Perhaps that is one pragmatic way to know when one unit is complete: when it's time for a test, or project, or some other culmination of learning in a formal assessment of learning. As we plan units, we should keep in mind an appropriate pace, not moving too quickly that students don't have the time needed to engage with the material, but not too slowly that they become bored either. Units are typically a few weeks to a month in length, but this depends on the particulars of the curriculum and the grade level of the students.

Lesson Plans

Unit plans can be further subdivided into smaller segments that we could call lessons. Lessons are typically one class meeting in length, but this depends on the particulars of the lesson. Some lessons require multiple days to complete, or some mini lessons might only need 15 minutes to master. Planning lessons is one of the central ways we enact the curriculum on a daily basis; this is where we most specifically bring together our knowledge of the students and our content knowledge with the teaching moves that will be most effective for helping these particular students master this particular content.

Here we must take care not to slide into the activity-orientation as we design learning activities. It can be easy to focus on fun activities and projects that we want students to have the opportunity to do that are connected to the big ideas of the unit. How can we ensure that students are working on meaningful learning that is appropriately challenging? We should plan lesson-level learning targets should for each lesson that are connected to content standards. Remember in a previous chapter that we described content standards as the signposts that serve as way-markers, so we know we are staying on the path of the curriculum.

Devising clear learning targets is key for avoiding the activity-focused approach to teaching. A learning target is usually framed as an "I can . . . " statement that gives voice to what students should know, understand, or be able to do by completing that lesson. Learning targets give us focus for our lessons, and help us to both choose learning activities that will help ensure students hit the target, as well as giving us ideas for the kind of evidence that will help us assess whether students have learned the key ideas for this lesson.

Consider that unit on chemical reactions I mentioned earlier. Some focused learning targets for each lesson can help us ensure we meet the broad learning goals for the unit. For example, the learning target for one lesson might be, "I can model what happens to the particles in a substance when a chemical reaction occurs." This target gives specific ideas for what could happen in the lesson: perhaps we would use modeling clay to represent atoms, and rearrange them to illustrate the chemical reaction, or sketch drawings of different types of reactions. This learning target might tie back to the broad goal of being able to identify chemical reactions as a step along the way to mastering that big idea. That's the real idea for lesson plans: they should be the building blocks within the unit that help ensure students learn the content for that segment of the overall curriculum.

One final thought on lesson plans: a great activity is not a lesson plan in and of itself! Lessons should have clear targets we are aiming for, and a clear plan for how we will know whether students have hit the target. Activity-focused teaching is a trap to be avoided, and ensuring that each lesson is framed by learning targets that connect back to the big ideas of the unit is a promising practice for eluding this trap.

Daily Plans

There is one other level of planning we should briefly discuss at this point. Teachers should have a sense of the flow of their whole day. This might look different at different grade levels. For example, at the high school and middle school level, teachers might be assigned to teach particular classes during specific blocks during the school day. For example, in my first teaching job, I taught middle school mathematics and a computer applications course for high schoolers. My day was dictated to me, in eight 40-minute chunks. I started the day with two eighth-grade math classes, then a high school computer applications class, then two sixth-grade math classes. After that came lunch and intramurals, followed by a free period to prepare. Finally, I closed out the day with two seventh-grade math classes. I did not have any say in the order of these classes, as they were arranged by our principal. Of course, there were always adjustments to be made; what happens when we have a half-day of school? Or an assembly to work around? Or a fire drill in the middle of one class? These sorts of events need to be planned around, of course. But the overall flow of the day was generally quite structured.

Elementary teachers, on the other hand, often have much more flexibility in the way they plan their days. They will have recess times and lunch to plan around, and usually some classes taught by specialist teachers, such as music, physical education, and art. But the rest of their day is often more malleable. How long should we spend on literacy? On math? On social studies and science? Laying out a reasonable daily plan is valuable, both for the teacher and the students alike. Early in your career, it is often helpful to reach out to seasoned colleagues as you are devising your daily plans, as they will have wisdom of experience and will be able to give you advice for creating plans that will work well for students at the grade level you are teaching.

Daily plans may look different in different schools, of course. There are lots of possible ways to structure the school day. Some schools use an odd-even schedule, where they have different schedules on different days of the week. Others use block schedules where you might have fewer, but longer class periods each day. Still others try to keep the daily schedule the same for a quarter, or trimester, or semester, and then completely change it the next term. There are strengths and weaknesses to each of these approaches, and there is not necessarily a "right" way to devise the school's schedule. But arranging your daily schedule within the school's schedule will help you manage the busyness of your work in planning for effective learning.

Taking stock of where we are at this point, we've thought through the importance of planning, and we've considered planning at different scales. We've discussed the role of broad goals as big ideas for structuring curriculum units, and the role of more specific learning targets for guiding the planning lessons. We've looked at plans as small as one school day, and as large as the whole school year. As we close out this chapter, let's think a little about the role of imagination in planning, and how effective planning fits in as part of teaching Christianly.

Lesson Planning as an Exercise in Imagination

You may remember that in the first chapter of this book, I introduced the idea that creativity is part of the work of imagination. I want to re-emphasize now that I believe *all* human beings are creative. You might not feel that you are very creative, but I want to challenge you to reimagine yourself as someone who creates things. Remember that we are made in God's image, and this means that we reflect what God is like. He is the Creator, and one way we bear his image is in our own capacity to be creative. And as a teacher, you will have many opportunities to be creative, not least of which is in your work of planning and designing instruction.

And so, considering how you are created to be, I want to challenge you to take a playful, generative, imaginative approach to your planning process. This does *not* mean that you need to reinvent the wheel for every lesson you teach! Some of the most creative teachers I know are the ones who are the most resourceful, always on the lookout for great ideas that they can borrow, adapt, and make their own. This is creative, imaginative work as well—adapting intriguing ideas about the content or innovative pedagogical approaches to make them work in your classroom, with your students, to engage them in deep, meaningful learning.

Be encouraged that the more you practice this kind of resourceful creativity, the more natural it becomes, and the more innovative ideas you'll have. Biochemist Linus Pauling once said, "The best way to have a good idea is to have a lot of ideas, and throw the bad ones away."[78] I love that strategy, and I've embraced it in my own teaching practice. I hope that hearing this gives you permission to have some bad ideas as you seek to play, and practice, and develop your teacher imagination. I know I've had plenty of terrible ideas in my career as a teacher! This sort of approach does demand a willingness to take reasonable risks, and it also requires a little resilience so you can bounce back from the ideas that don't work out quite as planned. But if you are prepared to step out in boldness, with a willingness to reflect on your practice and keep learning, I am confident that you'll find this approach a productive way to grow your imagination about your planning.

Always Becoming, Never Arriving

As we seek to teach Christianly, we can take a playful, creative attitude toward our planning. David Smith encourages Christian teachers to develop a faith-informed, imaginative approach to their teaching practices, saying:

> Attending to faith's role within our pedagogical world involves being able to imagine afresh, to see anew, and for this we need not so much to think harder as to engage in the practices that nurture Christian imagination. We need to invest in becoming people capable of imagining in Christian ways, of seeing our classrooms through the lenses of grace, justice, beauty, delight, virtue, faith, hope, and love.[79]

This is the sort of work of imagination I'm getting at here when it comes to planning. What is the deep learning you want your students to achieve? What should students carry with them when they leave your class?

My friend Darryl De Boer uses what he calls the "Rule of 60" as a way of helping teachers set meaningful goals for deep learning. Some learning is 60-minute learning; it might be helpful for today's class meeting, but perhaps students don't really need to know it any longer than that. Some learning is 60-day learning; students should know it at least until they take the final test or complete a project to demonstrate their learning. But some learning is 60-year learning, learning that will make an impact for the rest of their lives. The idea of the Rule of 60 is to try and imagine 60-year learning in your curriculum and focus the bulk of your plans to ensure that *this* is what students carry with them. How will the opportunities they have to learn in your classroom shape the people they are growing into, and how they live their lives into the future? How will the content, and the way you teach it impact their cognitive, social, emotional, and spiritual development? What a difference this kind of Christian imagination would bring as we plan for deep learning!

Questions for Reflection after Reading

1. In this chapter there is an emphasis on *ensuring* student learning through strong planning. How do you feel about the idea of "ensuring" students will learn?
2. What is a new idea that helped expand your imagination?
3. What challenged your thinking, or what question would you like answered?

Chapter 13

Getting Inside their Heads
The Most Mystical Part of Teaching

Taylor's Journal . . .

You know what? I. HATE. ASSIGNING. GRADES. I hate them! It is ridiculous to have to try and sum up all of a kid's learning with just one symbol. How can I accurately use a letter grade to capture everything Micah has learned this semester despite being out sick for two weeks? What if Charlie already knew everything I was planning to teach this semester—did he even learn anything from me?—and if he didn't learn anything, what grade should he get for putting in his time with me? How about Sara? She has come SO FAR . . . but if she doesn't yet meet the standard, what grade should she get? Can I grade on effort? Ugh, this is the worst part of the job for me.

    I think figuring out what my students actually are learning is the hardest thing about teaching. What did they know before they were in my class? What new things are they taking away from my lessons? Am I asking them the right questions on this test to truly discover what they know? Should I give them a project instead? Ooof . . . I have *more questions than answers, but I'm thinking that I need to overhaul my whole assessment system, because this feels broken.*

How Do We Know What They Know?

In some sense, teachers need to develop the ability to read minds. If our work is ensuring that students learn, we must somehow get inside their heads so that we can know what they know. I think that this is the most mystical part of teaching: how do you understand what someone else understands? In the last chapter, we considered how we can make plans that will ensure students will learn. In this chapter, let's turn our attention to another pressing question: how will we *know* that they have learned? This is an opportunity for us to develop our teacher imaginations to try and picture what is happening when we ask students to demonstrate their learning.

Let's pretend that you are given your choice of how you would display what you have learned about a topic. Do you have a strong preference for what you would do to illustrate your understanding? Would you rather take a test? Write an essay? Give a presentation? Would you do some sort of creative project to illustrate? There are lots of ways to show what we have learned![80]

While some people have strong preferences for ways to play to their strengths as they show what they know, for many of us, the answer to "Which way would you choose?" is probably, "It depends . . . " This is because there are different strengths and weaknesses in various ways of getting information about students' knowledge, skills, understanding, feelings, and beliefs. Sometimes the learning target will directly inform our approach. For example, if students are learning to write a five-paragraph essay in their language arts class, having them write an essay would almost certainly be the best way to make judgments about their mastery of this skill, right?

Other times, however, there are multiple approaches we could select from, and we should carefully match what we ask students to do to demonstrate their learning with the targets we are aiming for. For example, a presentation in front of the class is probably not the best way to check if students have mastered the basic facts of multiplication; this is almost certainly "too big" of an assignment for the scope of the learning target. Instead, a short quiz, or even a one-on-one check in with the teacher is probably better suited to this work. Likewise, a multiple-choice test is probably not the best way to determine if a student can light a Bunsen burner and safely heat a liquid in a test tube; an actual demonstration of these skills would be more appropriate. Right-sizing the work, and asking students to do the *right* work to provide evidence their learning are the key.

Evidence of Learning: Assessment and Evaluation

This whole idea of getting inside our students' heads to find evidence of learning is one of the three key things teachers do: planning, instruction, and assessment. When we are talking about assessment, we are thinking about evidence of learning, and how teachers can choose the best strategies for finding that evidence so they can document students' achievement. There is a little vocabulary we should clarify for thinking about this evidence; let's distinguish "assessment" and "evaluation."

Assessment is about collecting evidence. When we are assessing our students' learning, we are looking for information about what they know, what they understand, what they can do. Assessment is guided by learning targets; ideally, the targets we set will determine the kinds of evidence we are seeking. For example, if a learning target in a music class is, "I can play different rhythms on a percussion instrument," I suspect you can immediately start to imagine ways to assessing that target. Maybe you would hand each a student a tambourine or wood block and have them repeat a rhythmic pattern back to you. Perhaps you would have them play a rhythm game with a partner, and then demonstrate a rhythmic pattern to the whole group. This learning target is clear and direct; it suggests specific things to look for, but it also excludes things that we are *not* looking for in this lesson, such as singing a melody, or changing the volume of music, or modifying the tempo of the music. It's not that we would not include those things as part of the lesson, but they are not the evidence we are looking to assess, given this particular learning target.

In common English, we might use the words "assessment" and "evaluation" interchangeably. When it comes to teaching, however, we should distinguish these. Evaluation is about *measuring* students' learning. You can see the word "value" as the root word "evaluation," and this is the key idea of evaluation: we are making a value judgment about how much students have learned.[81] In terms of learning targets, evaluation might be a way of saying not just, "Did they hit the target?" but "How close to the bullseye did they get?" In practice, evaluation is generally about assigning a grade—a letter, a percentage, or some other symbol—to illustrate our measurement of how much students have learned.

Is it possible to evaluate learning without assessment? No. We need to have collected some evidence to measure it! But is it possible to assess learning without evaluation? This is a more complicated question. I think our human nature is to almost immediately snap to making judgments about the things we observe, so in that sense, we are certainly evaluating our students' work constantly. That said, if we define evaluation as "grading" student work, there are many times in which we might collect evidence about student learning without assigning a grade. In fact, I want to suggest that this is likely a practice worth pursing; we can often provide feedback on students' work-in-progress without giving summary judgement, and this will positively benefit their learning.

Different Roles of Assessment

Thinking through this relationship between assessment and evaluation is an opportunity for us to examine the different roles assessment plays as teachers do that mystical work of getting inside their students' heads. We should consider pre-assessment, summative assessment, and formative assessment.

Pre-assessment is just what it sounds like: assessment done prior to the work of teaching and learning. Pre-assessment is about finding out what students *already* know, understand, and can do before you begin teaching. Our students are not blank slates when they come into our classroom; they are knowledgeable, experienced human beings. Many students will almost certainly have some degree of understanding of the topics to be encountered in a new unit before you begin the teaching. Uncovering their current level of background knowledge will help you to be more effective in meeting students where they are and help ensure they will hit the learning targets.

Summative assessment is probably what immediately leaps to mind when you think about assessing learning—tests, projects, and presentations are almost always summative assessments. Summative assessments can best be thought of as assessments *of* learning: opportunities for students to summarize and synthesize the things they have learned at the end of a unit and put it on display for the teacher. Summative assessments are valuable for teachers to ensure that students have met all the learning targets for a unit.

Formative assessments, in contrast to summative assessments, can be thought of as assessments *for* learning. Formative assessments are ways of the teacher checking in on how students are understanding new ideas and how they are building new skills even as the learning is ongoing. As an analogy, think of a cook tasting the soup while it is simmering on the stove. This allows the cook to add a little salt or adjust the blend of seasonings so that it tastes just right before dinner is served. Formative assessment is just like that: checking in on how things are simmering along in the learning process. Summative assessment is the "dinner is served" judgment of the finished work. Formative assessments can take a multitude of different forms, from formal things like quizzes or writing assignments, to informal check-ins like questioning, journal entries, worksheets, and observation of skills being developed. I would argue that *anything* students do can be a formative assessment, because they all will give you some sense of what and how students are understanding the material.

Where does evaluation fit in to all of this? Remember that assessment is the collecting of evidence, and evaluation is making judgments about the evidence. So, evaluation happens all along the way! The teacher collects evidence in a pre-assessment and evaluates what they will need to do to ensure that their teaching will help students meet the learning targets. While the teaching is underway, formative assessments provide evidence that the teacher can use to evaluate their own performance as a teacher and evaluate how students are making progress towards the goals. At the end of a learning segment, summative assessments provide evidence the teacher can use to judge the overall learning for each student.

I use that word "judge" specifically. I believe that judging student learning is an essential part of our professional responsibilities as teachers. But also want to urge a little caution; I think some teachers can go overboard with emphasizing judgment of students' learning. We should not only value the summative product of their learning. We should also value the *process* of learning. And in this, I think that emphasizing formative assessment, and the feedback to students that should come with it is a more promising practice for us. Learning is a journey, and I believe that feedback along the way is a more impactful way to ensure growth in knowledge, deepening of understanding, and development of skills than just giving a summary judgment.

Correcting, Grading, Marking . . . Is There a Difference?

I want to think about feedback on student work specifically. How do we give useful feedback to students on their work while learning is still underway? The way we respond to student work matters.

I once was having a hallway conversation with two colleagues, and as it wrapped up, one of my colleagues sighed, "Well, I better get moving, I have papers to correct." The second colleague smiled: "It's funny to me that you call it 'correcting.' I call it 'grading.'" Then I was my turn to chuckle: "Ah, and I call it 'marking papers!'" My first colleague laughed: "Well, whatever we call it, I better get to it. That pile on my desk isn't getting any smaller while we are here visiting." And so, we each headed on our way to tackle our respective stacks of student work, but this brief exchange caught my imagination. Let's think about what might look different when it comes to what each teacher is actually doing when we describe our work as correcting, grading, or marking—and the strengths and weaknesses of each of these approaches.

Correcting

What does "correcting" imply when we are thinking about student work? If we are correcting their work, it suggests that we are looking for errors, noting them, and fixing them so the final work is "correct." There certainly is a benefit to this: students are going to make errors in their work from time to time, and making mistakes is a natural part of learning. Teachers *should* help students along the path to learning, and correcting errors is one way to do this.

However, it seems to me that the emphasis in the "correcting" approach to fix students work. I wonder if it might make sense to teach students to correct their own work? This might be more beneficial for them in the long run. Correcting students' errors is a valuable piece of providing them feedback on learning, but there is more to feedback than just catching mistakes.

Grading

"Grading" carries a stronger evaluative connotation, one that indicates there is a standard to be met, and that the teacher is making a professional judgment about whether students have met that standard. Grading is often quantitative work, where teachers calculate a score or a percentage, which makes it feel more objective and less subject to how the teacher might be feeling when working through the students' assignments. This might work reasonably well for some things, such as a worksheet of math exercises or vocabulary definitions, where there are clear right-or-wrong responses. But for much of the work we ask students to do, there is a range of "correctness" in the way they demonstrate their current understanding—it isn't all objective.

Some teachers still argue that grades are objective, because "everyone knows what a grade means." I once had a colleague who said, "When I'm grading, I can just tell an 'A' paper from a 'B' paper." I bristled at this idea. While we as teachers might have clear ideas of what the grade represents, this might not be clear *at all* to students. And does a "B" in one class mean the same thing as a "B" in another class?

Using a rubric can help to give clarity on what the grade means.[82] But even with a rubric, there may be concerns about using grades for giving feedback. How much information about the strengths and weaknesses of the work are really conveyed by just one letter or number? It seems like there is some nuance being left out of the feedback when we are using grades to communicate learning.

Marking

"Marking" papers might make you picture a teacher making checkmarks on a worksheet, and that is certainly part of the idea of marking papers. Maybe this is why the idea of "marking papers" is still part of my vocabulary; it's a carryover from my days of checking students' pencil-and-paper quizzes from my math classes or marking off items on a rubric to score lab reports in my science classes—actually making marks with pen on paper. Marking might work well for some kinds of assessments, but less well than others.

Marking can have a bit of a hands-off feeling though, as if the teacher is just a technician who is making tick-marks on a form, checking things off the to-do list. The connotation of marking can make the work of providing feedback seem more distant, or more abstract than either correcting or grading does. Correcting feels very close to students, with a teacher who cares deeply about students. Grading seems to really capitalize on the professionalism of the teacher. Marking seems a little colder and more clinical, as if there isn't much of a relationship there, and then we should rightly ask whether this is real feedback!

Feedbacking?

I would like to propose "feedbacking" as an alternative term to correcting, grading, or marking. I think this better gets at what we are really trying to do when we are assessing students' learning and evaluating their work. Feedback has a connotation of growth and learning. Rick Wormeli's definition for feedback is instructive; he suggests feedback is "telling students what they did . . . and helping them compare what they did with what they were supposed to do."[83] This helps keep the focus on the *learning*, rather than the "earning" of a grade.

It's not that teachers should never assign a grade; at this point, grades are still firmly part of school culture. But we should not confuse grading and feedback as being the same thing. Perhaps a better way of thinking about the role of feedback within an assessment and evaluation system is using data to make decisions: to what degree have students mastered this content? Are we ready to move on, or is some reteaching needed? And how are students perceiving their own learning? Feedback that is timely, specific, and actionable can help them move deeper in their understanding of the big ideas you are working to help them master.

Does Jesus Care about How I Grade My Students' Work?

When we are discussing assessment and evaluation of students learning, it might be easy for us to place most of the burden for the work of learning on students. This is right, to an extent; students certainly have a role to play in their own learning! But to place *all* the burden for learning on students is not just. After all, if students are not learning . . . and our role as teachers is to ensure that students learn . . . perhaps we should also take a hard look at ourselves if students are not performing to our expectations. What I mean by this is that while teachers certainly do have a professional responsibility to evaluate our students' work, perhaps we also should be equally self-critical and judge our own work as the teacher. If my students aren't learning, perhaps some self-reflection is in order!

It certainly is tempting to blame students when things aren't going well. I clearly remember a time relatively early in my teaching career that my eighth-grade science students performed very poorly on a test. In this case, the *whole class* did badly; many students failed, and even students who typically did relatively well in my class had underperformed. My immediate response after I had finished marking their tests was disgust—disgust with my students. I wanted to justify myself, so I said something like, "Well, they clearly did not study very hard for this test!" But within a few minutes, the reality of the situation crashed into me. If *all* my students did poorly perhaps the students were not the problem!

I started thinking through the test I had written and noticed several problems with it. Some of the questions I had devised were confusing. The way I had arranged vocabulary questions asked them to match definitions to terms, rather than terms to definitions—which is a much more cognitively demanding task. Several of the short essay questions I included were on topics that we had only touched on briefly in class and were not very closely related to the big ideas for the unit. My honest self-assessment: I wrote a bad test. It is no wonder students did not do well!

The hard part for me was humbling myself enough to confess my error to my students, but that is what I did. The next day, I admitted to them that I was first upset with them about how badly things had gone, but how I had quickly realized that the problem was not with them, but with me. We took time to go through the test together in class, and I pointed out the places where things had gone wrong, the bad design of some parts of the test, and how I had asked questions that were not well aligned to the big ideas. The students were incredibly gracious, and it ended up being a great opportunity to build relationships with my students and demonstrate how much I cared about them and about their learning.

I then asked them what we should do about this test, because I did not feel right about including it as part of their grade for the class. (They were relieved to hear it!) We brainstormed a bit, and in the end the students thought that retaking a revised test made the most sense for us. I agreed with them. So, I wrote a new test, and a few days later the students took it. Overall, most students did *much* better on the redo. This was an important lesson for me, and for my students too, I think. All too often teachers—and students—think of assessment as something done *to* students. This episode of my terrible test opened my eyes to the idea that assessment should be done *with* students, and *for* students. Rather than thinking of assessment as a "gotcha" or a way of punishing students for not having learned things, this unfortunate encounter pushed me toward thinking about the ways I might *bless* my students through my assessment practices.[84]

You might not think that the Christian faith has much to say about how teachers grade their students work, but I think that Jesus cares about even this mundane aspect of our work. All this talk of judgment in this chapter might remind you of Jesus's words in Matthew 7 where he says, "Do not judge."[85] That might make you think that we should take a light approach to evaluating students' work—after all, isn't Jesus saying we should *not* judge others?

In truth, I don't think that this is what Jesus is teaching here at all. Let's take that verse in context; Jesus goes on to say:

> Do not judge, or you too will be judged. For in the same way you judge others, you will be judged, and with the measure you use, it will be measured to you. Why do you look at the speck of sawdust in your brother's eye and pay no attention to the plank in your own eye? How can you say to your brother, "Let me take the speck out of your eye," when all the time there is a plank in your own eye? You hypocrite, first take the plank out of your own eye, and then you will see clearly to remove the speck from your brother's eye.[86]

I think what Jesus is really teaching here is that the *way* we judge matters. As I've previously noted, teachers have a professional responsibility to judge students' growth and learning. What Jesus is nudging us towards here is a self-reflective awareness of the ways we miss the mark. Teachers are not immune to plank-eye syndrome. If we are taking seriously the call to teach Christianly, let's exercise a little cautious self-awareness as we judge our students' work. Our students need grace in the same ways the you and I do.

Questions for Reflection after Reading

1. How does the idea of judging students as a professional expectation for you as a teacher make you feel? Why?
2. What is a new idea that helped expand your imagination?
3. What challenged your thinking, or what question would you like answered?

Chapter 14

Effective Instruction
Teaching like Jesus?

Taylor's Journal . . .

Today was one of those days where everything just "worked." I had taught this same lesson a few times in the past, and it never felt quite right. In the previous version, it was just a whole lot of me talking at the students . . . and they were bored. Honestly, I was bored too! So, this time I decided to try and re-configure the lesson into a sort of game.

Instead of me just telling them a lot of information, defining terms and giving them examples, I turned the lesson around. I started with the examples, and I asked them to try and sort them into categories. Pretty quickly, they were arguing—in the best way—about what kinds of categories these different items could be sorted into. They were making claims, giving their evidence, making counter-claims, and really thinking deeply. As they were leaving our classroom today, even Drew was smiling. I said, "It almost looks like you were having fun in class today, Drew." He knew I was teasing him, and his quick response was, "Well, it was actually fun today."

I was absolutely delighted that this little change-up worked out so well. And if I can even get Drew to admit he enjoyed class today, well . . . it was a good day of teaching today! Getting a little more intentional about being playful really paid off.

Was Jesus an Effective Teacher? (Don't Worry, I'm Not Sacrilegious . . .)

Who is Jesus to you? I believe that Jesus Christ is the sovereign king of the cosmos,[87] present at creation,[88] the redeemer of all things,[89] and coming again to put a final end to sin, and evil, and death.[90] I say all of this because there are some people who want to somehow suggest that Jesus was just a good, moral teacher who had a lot of wise sayings, and did some good things while he was here on Earth. But I want to be clear that viewing Jesus as *only* a teacher is not giving him his due as King of Kings and Lord of Lords; I believe that Jesus is the very Son of God![91]

That said, Jesus *was* a teacher. Throughout the Gospels, Jesus is addressed as "rabbi," or "teacher," or even "good teacher" many times, so it's clear that Jesus was viewed by the people around him as a teacher. And he *did* teach; he preached sermons, he told parables, he gave encouragement and guidance to his disciples, he debated with religious leaders, he expounded upon Scripture in the synagogues. Jesus *was* a teacher.

But was Jesus an *effective* teacher? (Please hear me out; really, I'm not being sacrilegious!) If you read through the Gospel stories, there are many examples of Jesus's disciples *completely missing* his message and ministry. They often did not catch the significance of his miracles. They regularly seemed to misunderstand the point of his parables. The disciples squabbled amongst themselves about the meaning of his words, and he frequently had to reteach and re-explain. Maybe you too are now wondering if perhaps Jesus just wasn't that good at teaching?

But here's the truth: in our work as teachers, we don't always see immediate success. Some of our work is planting seeds—seeds that may sprout and bear fruit *much* later on. I believe this was the truth for Jesus's teaching. In fact, Jesus's teaching was exactly what his disciples needed to equip them to carry on his ministry after his death, resurrection, and ascension. They did not immediately understand the implications of what he was teaching them, but eventually it all became clear to them. As the apostle John relayed it, "At first his disciples did not understand all this. Only after Jesus was glorified did they realize that these things had been written about him and that these things had been done to him."[92]

We can take encouragement from this, I think. There may be times that it seems we are just scattering seeds. But purposeful planning, and care in the way execute those plans as our lessons unfold can equip students in ways that will bear fruit in both the short and longer term. Let's keep in mind the Rule of 60 and focus on that 60-year learning: what will students carry with them for the rest of their lives? To ensure students learn, let's be very mindful of our pedagogical moves.

Pedagogical Moves: What Are You Doing, and Why Are You Doing It?

Every teacher has "moves" that they utilize in the classroom as they are teaching students. Think about your own teachers that you've had throughout your schooling: can you think of catchphrases, or quirky behaviors, or just general ways of doing things those particular teachers used regularly? Those are all examples of what I mean by pedagogical moves: they are the teaching strategies and approaches toward the curriculum that we select to help our students learn the content.

Our pedagogical moves run the range from small-scale, just-in-the-moment decisions about how to respond to a student's question when it is asked, all the way up to massive, "how am I going to be as a teacher" approaches. Our moves include our physical movement around the classroom, the way we prompt students to speak (or be quiet), the ways we present content, the kinds of assignments we devise, the way we provide feedback to students, the kinds of questions we ask, the way we distribute and collect materials, the way we make groups, the technologies we use (or exclude), and many, many more. The next time you are watching a teacher at work in their classroom, try and take note of all the teaching moves they use. I suspect you will be amazed—and perhaps a little surprised—at just how many instructional decisions teachers make in a single class meeting. It's no wonder teachers go home tired at the end of the school day!

The real questions for us to consider as we think about our teaching moves are "What am I doing?" and "*Why* am I doing this?" If we are serious about ensuring that students learn, we need to choose our pedagogical moves with care and intentionality. But with all the possible teaching approaches we could choose from, how do we begin to winnow down to the most effective strategies? I think there are five lenses we can use to help us give better answer to the "what" and "why" of our teaching methods.

The first lens is *student needs*. Previously in this book, we spent some time thinking about learner development and learner diversity. Considering what we know about the typical development of our students can give us guidance about what moves are most appropriate for ensuring they will learn. While there certainly are moves that work just as well for six-year-olds and sixteen-year-olds, there are some approaches that will be more developmentally appropriate for younger students, and other approaches better for older students. We should also take into account the diversity of the students in our class and acknowledge that different students will need different things to be successful in learning.[93] If we keep in mind students' needs in terms of their development and diversity, our moves will almost certainly be better suited for ensuring learning.

The second lens to consider is the *demands of the content*. In a previous chapter we were thinking through pedagogical content knowledge: the idea that we use different methods for teaching different disciplines. Understanding that teaching art is different than teaching science, which is different than teaching physical education, which is different than teaching literature means we must choose the right techniques for conveying the content in that discipline. This does not mean that there aren't moves that transcend disciplinary boundaries; there certainly are methods that work well in many different content areas! The idea here is that there are some methods that are uniquely well-suited for particular content, and we should be mindful about the difference between teaching math and music, for example.

A third lens to inform our teaching moves is *educational research*. I've sometimes heard people put down "research-based strategies," but we should be very careful to not be so quick to dismiss the role of research in education. There are some teaching methods that are, simply put, more effective for ensuring that students will truly learn.[94] Research-based strategies can take on a variety of characteristics, and some are discipline-specific, while others can be readily used in many different content areas. Again, the key idea here is being intentional about selecting strategies that are more likely to help students learn. It's not that strategies that don't have deep research behind them are ineffective, but rather that they might be *less* effective. And we should also consider a further outcome of much research in education: teachers tend to teach as they were taught. This means that unless they very intentionally seek to learn and practice different teaching methods, teachers may miss out on strategies that might be more powerful for ensuring students learn.[95]

A fourth lens we should explore is the *space we teach within*. Different classrooms have different strengths and weaknesses. The way a classroom is furnished, and even the way the furnishings are arranged can make some teaching methods easier or more difficult. Consider, for example, the difference of arranging student desks in rows facing in one direction, versus arranging them in pods of 4 students facing each other, versus arranging them in a large circle. What kinds of teaching methods are harder to implement, and which are easier in each of these arrangements? In the first arrangement with the desks all facing forward individual, teacher-directed work is usually the priority. In the second arrangement with pods of students, collaborative learning strategies would work very well. And the third arrangement, with students all facing each other, discussion and debate would be much easier to facilitate. We can't always adapt our classroom spaces so easily; I once had to teach a lecture-based class in a science lab, which was not ideal. Or imagine teaching an art class in a room with a carpeted floor and no sinks for cleaning up; that would likely change what kinds of learning activities you would plan for students to do, wouldn't it?

A final lens to consider is *teacher preference*. While I'm not sure there is a ranking to the other four lenses in terms of their importance in a hierarchy of decision-making, I am saving this one for last. Teacher preference *is* an important lens for choosing teaching methods, but the other four are almost certainly more important. But as I say this, we should take our own preferences into account as we choose our pedagogical moves—there are some teaching strategies that are simply more in line with our personal style in the classroom. For example, as student, I strongly disliked it when teachers would cold-call on us to respond to their questions. This is actually a highly effective teaching strategy, but I rarely use it, because I remember that feeling of being called-out in front of the class so well, and it makes me feel uncomfortable. That said, I will use this strategy from time to time, but only when paired with a few other strategies to make it more in line with my classroom style: I normalize "passing" (that is, giving students the opportunity to pass temporarily) or using "turn and talk" before calling on students (that is, giving them the chance to think out loud with a partner before being expected to share out with the whole class). Back in chapter

1, we considered Parker Palmer's idea that "you teach who you are." We should know who we are, and we should let our individual identities inform our classroom moves.

Thinking through these five lenses for *every* decision you make in the classroom is not feasible, of course. There are many times you will have to make snap decisions about how to address a situation that comes up while you are teaching a lesson. My point here is that there are heuristics we can utilize to help us ensure that the methods we are selecting to use will be more impactful for ensuring learning. Coming back to those two key questions, we must continue to ask ourselves, "What am I doing?" and "Why am I doing this?" Our answers to these questions matter greatly and will help us make pedagogical decisions, and the way you answer these probably indicates more about your personal philosophy of education than perhaps any other questions you might ask. All your instructional moves flesh out your philosophy of education and illustrate what you believe about your role as a teacher.

This might seem daunting, as though the teaching moves you choose will make or break your success in educating your students. We *should* take our moves seriously and plan them out carefully. But we should also recognize that teachers often must respond and even change course very quickly depending on how things are unfolding while the lesson is being taught. In these moments, we won't have time to think through all these lenses; rather, we often will make snap judgments on the fly.

But here is some good news: as you grow in experience, much of this kind of pedagogical decision-making becomes more automatic. Being very intentional at carefully choosing your moves early on in your career as a teacher sets you up for longer term success as you continue to practice these moves over time. And for some more good news: you can always keep learning and keep on trying new things in your teaching practice. Just because you try something once and don't get the results you were hoping for doesn't make you a bad teacher. It might just mean you need to learn a little more about that strategy, or practice more, or try a new strategy entirely. There are always more opportunities to grow and develop in your teaching practice!

Should I Just Tell Them, or Let Them Figure It Out for Themselves?

Let's recap where we are at the moment in terms of our discussion of instructional methods. We've noted that there is a wide range of possible teaching methods we can choose from, and that if we are serious about ensuring that our students learn, we need to choose our pedagogical moves with care and intention. The two big questions we're really asking when we think about these moves are, "What am I doing? and "Why am I doing this?" We also looked at five lenses we can use to help us make better instructional decisions to ensure that our students will learn. We also noted that teachers make small-scale instructional decisions on the fly all the time, but these in-the-moment decisions are contextualized within a broader framework of our personal philosophy of education. So now let's zoom all the way out for a moment and consider the most basic approaches to teaching and learning.

All of the wide array of different teaching methods we might choose from eventually funnel back into two general approaches to teaching. These two approaches can be used at any grade level, and in any content area; they are that broad and overarching. I call these two basic approaches the Just Tell Them approach and the Let Them Figure It Out approach. Let's briefly compare these approaches.

The "Just Tell Them" Approach

The Just Tell Them approach is just what it sounds like: the teacher passes on knowledge to the students. The teacher's role in this approach is the "knower" and the "teller": the teacher knows the content to be taught and tells this information to the students. The students' role is more passive, as a receiver of the information from the curriculum.

You probably are already picturing a teacher standing in front of the classroom and lecturing when I describe the Just Tell Them approach, and you're right that lecture is a go-to teaching method. But there are many others that could be utilized here as well, including textbook readings, instructional videos, worksheets, demonstrations, teacher questioning and student recitation, teacher moderated discussions, storytelling, guest speakers, and modeling of techniques students will need to use in their independent work. Hands-on activities can be part of the Just Tell Them approach as well: I think of the "cookbook" style lab activities I often used with my middle school science classes to ensure they would observe specific phenomena, for example.

The main idea of the Just Tell Them approach is *teacher direction*. In fact, this approach is often labeled "direct instruction." I want to be very clear that this is not a bad way to teach; direct instruction is often very effective! Also of note: direct instruction often goes hand-in hand with good organization.[96] Your class presentations can be carefully planned out ahead of time. Thoughtful, thought-provoking questions can be crafted before the discussion begins. Materials can be laid out in advance which can lead to easier classroom management—or at least the perception that this is the case. And direct instruction is often a very efficient way to teach; we can convey relatively larger amounts of content in a shorter period of time when we use the Just Tell Them approach.

On the other hand, there are some potential downsides of this approach that we should be cautious about. I already noted that direct instruction gives the perception of easier classroom management; I am not sure this is always the case. The teacher is controlling the content, but this also means the students often have less personal involvement with the material, which can mean boredom is more likely as an outcome. Our role as teachers is not to entertain our students, it is to educate them! But at the same time, I sometimes wonder just how much learning is taking place when students are not actively engaged in class.

The "Let Them Figure It Out" Approach

In contrast, the Let Them Figure It Out approach demands active engagement on the part of the students. The teacher's role in this approach shifts to much more of a facilitator. This is not to say that the teacher does not know the content (they should!) But the teacher shifts from telling students the information to arranging things in the classroom so that students will *encounter* the information for themselves.

Hearing that the teacher's role is more of a facilitator probably gives you a very different picture of what is happening in the classroom as opposed to a teacher-directed lecture. Cooperative learning and student collaboration are key characteristics in the Let Them Figure It Out approach. Some common methods would include student research projects, inquiry-based investigations in which students seek out answers to their own questions, interpreting data and making inferences, problem solving (of authentic problems, not just math exercises out of a textbook, for example), book circles, debates, learning centers, and student-led discussions. I should be clear here that in each of these kinds of learning activities, the teacher still has a role to play. The teacher's role, however, is more about arranging for the learning to happen, rather than directing every aspect of what happens in the classroom.

The main idea for the Let Them Figure It Out approach then is student initiative. In contrast to the direct instruction approach, we could consider this "indirect instruction," where the teacher is confident enough—and humble enough—to get out of the driver's seat and invite students to take an active role in their own education. This is scary for many teachers, and not just the ones new to the profession! But the upside is that students almost always enjoy their schoolwork more when they have the opportunity for more active involvement![97]

And here we find the biggest potential downside as well: what happens if students *don't* take initiative in their own learning? If the lesson you have planned hinges on students asking their own questions and going out seeking answers, what happens to learning if they don't ask good questions? What happens to the debate if the students don't buy in to the topic? What happens to the collaborative project if students refuse to cooperate with each other? Perhaps it's no wonder that even seasoned teachers sometimes worry about using indirect teaching approaches.

Finding Some Balance?

Both the Just Tell Them and Let Them Figure It Out approaches have merit. Both approaches also have challenges. So, while many of us might gravitate towards one approach or the other, a wise teacher will include a variety of different methods—some more direct, and some more indirect—in their repertoire of pedagogical moves. There are a variety of reasons why we might tend towards some approaches over others. The lenses we discussed previously are helpful for discerning some of these: the age of the students we teach, the specific content areas we have been prepared to teach, and our own preferences as learners (and thus as teachers) are all powerful shaping influences on the pedagogical moves we tend towards using. And the methods that have been modeled for us are also a big influence. We must be aware of these influences, and how they might be impacting our decision-making for which moves are utilizing.

Intentionally planning to incorporate a mixture of teaching strategies may be an antidote to counter the weaknesses of both the Just Tell Them and the Let Them Figure It Out approaches. A good rule of thumb is what I will call the 60 Percent Strategy: no teaching strategy, no matter how effective it may be, should be used more than 60 percent of the time.[98] This is not a hard-and-fast rule that we have to slavishly follow, but I think it's good advice. Think of your own school experiences; did you ever have a teacher who over did it with collaborative learning, to the point that you got sick of it? Or maybe a teacher who lectured every day, to the point where you dreaded going to that class? Using the 60 Percent Strategy can help with finding a little balance. And with more balance, we'll be able to capitalize on the strengths of various pedagogical moves.

Instructional Moves, Teacher Beliefs, and a Christian Imagination

One of the very real challenges in all of this is ensuring that the instructional methods we decide to use in our classrooms align with our beliefs. There will almost certainly be times when you realize that what you (say you) believe, and what you are doing in your classroom are running contrary to one another. That is an uncomfortable place to be, speaking from personal experience. A big part of the problem is that teachers never have enough time to do everything that they want to do. There is always more that could be done! And because of the stress and pressure, there are many times that we must make pragmatic decisions as we plan, instruct, and assess that might not line up very well with our stated beliefs. Our instructional moves might belie our "real" beliefs—the ones we put into action. When we become aware of a mismatch between what we are doing and our professed beliefs, this can add to the stress.

Teaching is hard work in any circumstance, after all. And trying to authentically live your calling as a faithful follower of Jesus in your classroom might feel like an additional burden rather than a blessing. But take heart; we always have a chance to keep learning, to keep growing, to keep expanding our imagination. Let's remember that we never "arrive" as teachers. Learning to teach Christianly is a long process of becoming.

Part of this process of becoming is learning to better understand ourselves as teachers. In terms of our focus in this chapter on instruction, this means we need to understand why we might tend to gravitate towards certain teaching methods and avoid others. But we should also be mindful of the possibilities of gaps between what we say we believe and what we do. Let's commit to imagining better ways for us to more fully live out our calling to follow Jesus in our work as teachers. And let's also recognize that we are each a work in progress: thanks be to God that he is not finished with us yet!

Questions for Reflection after Reading:

1. When you think about your own preferences as a learner, what pedagogical moves seem like they will be most natural and comfortable for you as a teacher?
2. What is a new idea that helped expand your imagination?
3. What challenged your thinking, or what question would you like answered?

Chapter 15

Joy on the Journey

Why We Never "Arrive" at Teaching Christianly

Taylor's Journal . . .

I'm really grappling with the implications of my faith for my teaching practice. I always have kind of thought, "Well, I'm a Christian, and I'm a teacher . . . so I guess I'm a Christian teacher, right?" But I was talking with Deb about this after school, and she said something that really challenged me. She also takes her faith seriously, and it's great to have a colleague who is also interested in seeing her work through a faith-informed lens. We were talking about the way she is rearranging the furniture in her room, to try and get her students to interact in more authentic conversations about what they are reading. I was helping her move the desks from rows into pods. And suddenly she asked me a weird question: "Taylor, do you think Jesus cares about how the desks are arranged in your classroom?" I stopped in my tracks. She followed up with, "That seems like kind of a silly thing for Jesus to care about, doesn't it?" and changed the subject.

But the more I've been thinking about this, the more convinced I am that Jesus really does care about the way the *desks are arranged in my classroom. Even that relatively small decision shows something about what I believe . . . and how I'm trying to line up what I believe with what I do as a teacher. And right now, all I'm seeing is how wide the gap is between what I say I believe, and what I am actually doing! I have more work ahead of me, I think.*

Teaching Christianly—the Redux

We are nearing the end of our journey together, but I want to call you back to something we discussed early on in this book, when I first introduced the idea of "teaching Christianly." You may remember the language lesson about the difference of thinking about the word "Christian" in its noun, adjective, and adverb forms? You'll recall that I love the word Christian as a noun: I *am* a "little Christ!" But when we start to apply the word Christian to teachers and the work of teaching, I wanted to bring in a little more nuance to see the difference between thinking of myself as "a Christian teacher," and considering my work as "teaching Christianly."

Using Christian as an adjective, we might think of it this way: I am a Christian, and I am a teacher . . . doesn't that mean I am a "Christian teacher"? While I certainly could describe myself this way, I am not sure this is the most helpful depiction. What do I mean by being a Christian teacher? That I am a teacher who goes to church on Sundays? That I am a teacher who quote Scripture in class? That I am a teacher who views my students as individuals uniquely created in the image of God? That I am a teacher who treats each of my students with dignity and respect? That I am a teacher who intentionally aligns my curriculum to biblical principles? That I am a teacher who seeks to win students as disciples of Jesus? Just what does "Christian" mean, when applied as an adjective to the teacher? Using "Christian" as an adjective is complicated!

But what if we use the adverb form instead? Rather than describing myself as a Christian teacher, what if I describe my work as "teaching Christianly?" What if I think about the work of teaching as a way of working out my own discipleship, of answering God's calling in my life, of seeking to give God glory through the work I do in my classroom? Does that bring a different perspective on my approach to the work? I believe this shifts the attention from *what* I am doing to *how* and *why* I am doing it that way. As John Van Dyk puts it,

> Teaching, like all other human activity oppressed by sin, cries out for redemption ... Your task, as a Christian teacher, is not simply to teach, but to teach Christianly. In response to God's calling, your work as a teacher is to be transformed into a redemptive activity.[99]

What an awesome thought! You and I have the blessing—and challenge—of reimagining the work of teaching as something done for the good of our students, for the good of the world, and to the glory of God! Utilizing the adverb form of "Christian" helps us set a direction for our work—teaching Christianly must point towards teaching in such a way that we are demonstrating we are being "little Christs," working towards the renewal and restoration of all things.

Different Views of Teaching Christianly

But here we arrive at a bit of a quandary. Do all Christian teachers see this work of following Jesus in the classroom the same way? Nope! There are many different views that different Christian educators might take towards the work of teaching Christianly.[100] Let's explore a few of these.

Devotional Activities as Teaching Christianly

Some Christians in education emphasize devotional activities as the key idea for how faith impacts teaching. In this view of teaching Christianly, activities such as prayer, reading the Bible, and singing Christian songs are the essential markers for how faith is illustrated in your teaching practice. In the extreme case, these kinds of devotional activities are simply tacked on to a "normal" school day—as if the rest of the school day is "school" but we are somehow making it Christian by adding on these kinds of practices of Christian spirituality. The potential problem with this approach is that views Christian practices as something that can be bolted on to our teaching, as something external to the work. From this view, "teaching" is one thing, and "faith" is another, and they are held as separate.

My concerns with this approach are twofold. First, this approach is very dualistic. That is, it separates the world in a way that suggests some things are "secular" while other things are "sacred"—even our time, which can be devoted to God, or not. In this approach, the devotional activities are viewed as sacred, but the rest of the work of teaching is somehow less than devoted to God. I find this problematic, because I believe that Christ rules over all things—there is no part of this world that is outside the scope of his reign! And if this is true, we can't really separate some things as devoted to God and other things as "secular."[101] Secondly, in this approach, teaching Christianly can only happen in faith-based non-public schools, as public schools in our pluralistic culture cannot take on this sort of sectarian approach. I find this problematic, because I know many Christian educators who take their faith very seriously who have been called to serve in public schools. I certainly want Christian teachers serving as salt and light in every school!

Modeling Christlike Behaviors as Teaching Christianly

Along these lines of salt and light comes another view of teaching Christianly. Some Christians in education emphasize modeling Christian behaviors and attitudes for students as the central means by which their faith impacts their teaching. This is admirable! Living out a Christian life is what we are called to do—not just in our vocations, but in *all* parts of our life. And serving as a model to young people about how to do this certainly is important and valuable. Demonstrating the Fruit of the Spirit in action certainly is a central part of Christian faith![102] And there definitely are specific virtues that can and should be modeled to young people: compassion, respect, patience, delight, wonder, self-restraint, humility, diligence, and more should all be illustrated and encouraged.

My concern with reducing teaching Christianly to just modeling Christian behaviors and attitudes is this: if you look at that list of virtues I mentioned . . . aren't these characteristics that *all* teachers should be modeling to their students, regardless of their faith commitments? I am not convinced that these are uniquely "Christian" characteristics. Certainly, Christian teachers *should* be modeling these sorts of behaviors and attitudes, as should all teachers!

Infusing a Christian Perspective as Teaching Christianly

So perhaps there is something more than attitudes and behaviors . . . like a Christ-centered perspective? Some Christians in education emphasize providing a biblical perspective on the subject matter as the essential way their faith impacts their teaching. Allowing the light of Scripture to illuminate our approach toward the content we are teaching is certainly an important part of living out our faith as Christian teachers. Helping students understand that God created all things and called them "good" is marvelous. Helping students come to see the brokenness we experience in our lives as pervasive effects of sin in our world is indispensable. Helping students celebrate the redemption that comes through Christ, and the way we are invited to work towards the renewal of all things is wonderful. Any topic we see in the curriculum can be viewed through this lens—and Christian teachers have a tremendous opportunity to help their students come to understand the contours of a biblical perspective in this way.

Valuable as it is to bring a Christian perspective to the curriculum, I have three brief concerns with this approach. First, I wonder sometimes about this kind of perspectivalism, and how it plays out in different subject areas. It might seem easier to do this kind of perspective-seeking in subjects like history or science. But how about teaching grammar or geometry? I think we often kind of lamely put a "Well, God created an orderly universe, didn't he?" sort of perspectival label on some subjects—which is not wrong, per se, but feels sort of weak, doesn't it? Secondly, I again worry about Christian teachers in public schools. Can they give full-voiced explanations of a Christ-centered perspective in the schools they are called to serve? Probably not, but I do not think this means they cannot teach Christianly in those settings. Finally, I wonder about whether teaching a biblical perspective without any opportunity to *practice* it makes an actual difference for students. Does learning *about* restoration have the same impact as *practicing* restoration? Adding in a Christ-centered perspective alone may not be enough.

Doing Service Projects as Teaching Christianly

In response to that concern about practicing faith, some Christians in education picture teaching Christianly as engaging students in doing service projects. Service is central to the life of faith, after all. In the book of James we read, "What good is it, my brothers and sisters, if someone claims to have faith but has no deeds? Can such faith save them?"[103] The implication is that we live out our faith in our actions. Jesus himself, when asked the question about how to inherit eternal life responded by telling the story of the Good Samaritan, which is a story that fundamentally suggests that serving others sacrificially is the greatest illustration of what it means to love others. Jesus ends the story by telling his audience, "Go and do likewise."[104] We certainly are called to put our faith into action by serving!

Engaging students in acts of service is clearly valuable, and we should consider ways for students to experience these kinds of formational learning experiences. My concern with this approach is not so much the service opportunities in and of themselves. Rather, I wonder about what this approach suggests about the rest of the school experience. Does this mean that if there isn't a service component, the curriculum is pointless? I think that expecting every unit to culminate in a service project is problematic in that it can soften the curriculum—not every topic to be studied has a natural connection to service. Requiring service as an outgrowth of the curriculum (particularly when the curriculum connections are shaky) might actually have the opposite effect on students of what is intended.

Rigor and Discipline as Teaching Christianly

Perhaps in response to this kind of worry about softening the curriculum, some Christians in education view teaching Christianly as strong academic rigor and tough classroom discipline. I love the idea of high expectations for students! Schools are academic institutions first and foremost, and we are in the work of education. So it goes that emphasizing academic attainment and instilling the discipline needed to achieve it are worthy goals for schools. I see this approach most often in Christian academies that advertise the link between taking their faith seriously and the educational outcomes they can achieve in terms of students' learning and behavior. I liken this to Jesus's teaching about the most important commandment in the Law: "Love the Lord your God with all your heart and with all your soul and with all your mind and with all your strength."[105] Loving God with all our mind—and the academic achievement that that can illustrate this love—is part of our calling. Loving God with all our strength—and the discipline it takes to do this to the best of our ability—is part of our calling.

And yet, this approach troubles me as well. Is academic excellence all there is to living our faith in the classroom? Is holding high expectations for student behavior central to a Christ-centered way of life? If we reduce teaching Christianly to just rigorous academics and tough discipline, I fear we are missing out on the heart and soul of the Gospel message.

Evangelism as Teaching Christianly

Aha! So, if we are intent on the heart and soul of the Gospel, perhaps we should think about possibilities Christian teachers have to share that Gospel message with young people? Some Christians in education picture teaching Christianly as primarily about evangelizing students. Young people spend significant time with their teachers, and in this view, Christian educators should carefully consider the opportunities this may provide for them to live out the Great Commission. After his resurrection, Jesus met with his disciples and specifically commanded them to "go and make disciples of all nations, baptizing them in the name of the Father and of the Son and of the Holy Spirit, and teaching them to obey everything I have commanded you."[106] Some Christian educators take this commission with them into their classrooms, seeking opportunities to share the good news with their students. This is beautiful, and I would heartily encourage Christians to always be ready to share the gospel and in any situation as the Spirit leads them.

You might then be surprised to hear that I have concerns with this approach. My chief concern is about the role of the teacher; as a teacher, your primary role is to educate. If you can share the good news explicitly, by all means you should do this! But our primary work as teachers—even as Christian teachers—is to *teach*. Shifting all the focus towards evangelism minimizes the importance of a holistic education by narrowing the teacher's role to just one aspect of Christian teaching.

Imitating Jesus as the "Master Teacher" as Teaching Christianly

Perhaps a broader view then is needed? What if we broaden our view to following Jesus himself? Some Christians in education view teaching Christianly as following the example of Jesus, the "master teacher." Jesus certainly was a teacher! The books of Matthew, Mark, Luke, and John capture many of Jesus's teachings on a wide variety of topics. Reading through the Sermon on the Mount[107] is almost unsettling in how direct he is in his teaching about all sorts of topics, from marriage, to prayer, to making oaths, to lust, to trusting God's providence for our needs. Jesus's many parables stretch our imaginations of the upside-down nature of what the kingdom of God really looks like. Even Jesus's acts of healing and other miracles are often accompanied by words of instruction. And yet, when I hear teachers say they want to "teach like Jesus," I confess that I get a very specific picture in my minds-eye. How did Jesus teach? He chose twelve students, and then had them spend three years hiking with him around the Judean countryside while he told stories about the kingdom. (For some of us, that might sound like the ideal teaching situation . . . and for others, perhaps the worst we can imagine!) Those disciples had a close-up look at Jesus all along the way, and had the benefit of deep relationships with him, and yet it seems that they constantly misunderstood Jesus's teaching. The four Gospels record so many examples of the disciples missing the mark, it might start to seem that Jesus was not all that effective as a teacher! I truly don't mean to sound sacrilegious as I say this, but if you spent three years with a small group of students and they did not understand what you were teaching them . . . well, we would probably wonder about your pedagogy too, wouldn't we?

All joking aside, I think there is a concern with the idea that we should simply "teach like Jesus" to teach Christianly. The point of the Gospel isn't to illustrate good pedagogy, after all. Truly, it isn't until after his death, resurrection, and ascension that Jesus's teaching seems to have suddenly clicked for his disciples, and after that, they were completely transformed.[108] And what made it click? The coming of the Holy Spirit! Perhaps we should not think too highly of ourselves that we might be able to "teach like Jesus" when it was the animating work of the Spirit that brought about the life-changing results of Jesus's teaching. While Jesus *was* a teacher, we do well to remember that his primary role is to be our Redeemer. We cannot take on that role!

Being Non-Reductionistic

There are certainly many different perspectives on what teaching Christianly might look like. As we walked through these varied viewpoints, I suspect that at least one or two of them might have seemed attractive to you. And yet, I also raised cautions about each of them. What are we to do with this?

I think it's important to recognize that none of these stances toward teaching Christianly I've described is *wrong*. We should only call it "wrong" if a teacher is deliberately trying to divorce their faith life from their teaching practice. In fact, there is much worth celebrating in each of these approaches! In every case, teachers who would hold that viewpoint are taking their Christian faith very seriously and seeking to apply it to their vocation.

Rather than "wrong," we might consider these different viewpoints as *inadequate*, or *incomplete*. The technical term that a philosopher would use is *reductionistic*. That is, each of these views reduces the whole truth of teaching Christianly to just one aspect and suggests that one aspect is the whole truth.

A non-reductionistic approach would have to be bigger and more encompassing than any of these ideas I've discussed. It would have to be bigger even than the sum of all these different views on teaching Christianly I've laid out here. It is nothing less than a total commitment to following Jesus through your work as a teacher. A non-reductionistic approach toward teaching Christianly is very hard to encapsulate, because it is an all-of-life sort of approach!

What Do You (Say You) Believe?

When I'm completely honest, this all-of-life approach to living out our faith in the classroom and out is a little scary to me. Can I *actually* do this? And what if I don't, or can't? Here is the good news: Jesus loves you. In fact, he delights in you! Any steps you take towards more fully living out your faith in him—including your teaching practice—are things he celebrates with joy. The truth is, on this side of glory, we aren't always going to get it right. But we must to keep striving towards more authentically teaching Christianly, day by day.

While I know that Jesus loves me, and I am seeking to faithfully follow him more and more, here is the trouble for me: I know that what I say and what I do don't always line up very well. I am still a work in progress, and sometimes the mismatch between my words and actions seems like an insurmountable problem. I am painfully aware of the admonishment found in chapter 3 of the book of James, which says "Not many of you should become teachers, my fellow believers, because you know that we who teach will be judged more strictly."[109] We teachers *are* held to a high standard; we *are* judged strictly. The gap between what I say and what I do are sometimes frighteningly large, and my awareness of this causes me some shame.

For example, I often say things like, "I believe my students are uniquely created as God's image-bearers with unique gifts, and talents, and strengths." But do I truly live out this belief in my teaching? Because if I just lump the students together as "the class" and sort of teach towards the middle . . . my actions and professed beliefs don't really line up very well, do they? Or how about grading student work? I can say things like, "I hate letter grades, because I think they are subjective, and I don't think averaging grades is fair to the process of learning." But what if I find myself in a school system that demands a letter grade or percentage score at the end of the term to sum up students' achievement? If I wind up tallying points and averaging a grade, my actions show my stated beliefs to be false, or at least weak.

These are just a few examples; I suspect that if you think about the things your teachers have said and done over your years in school you could come up with a long list of examples of these kinds of gaps as well. Teachers, despite their best intentions, are also affected by sin, and we can't always get things right. The gap between what we say we believe and what we actually do is one clear way that this is illustrated, perhaps on a daily basis! What are we to do about this?

Shrinking the Gap Between Theory and Practice

Maybe it makes sense for us to talk about this in terms of "theory" and "practice." For our purposes, let's define "theory" as "the things (you say) believe." Let's define "practice" as "the things you actually do." Teachers can describe a lot of things in theory; the topics we have discussed in this book are rooted in sound educational theory, such as developmental theories, and learning theories, and research-based best practices for instruction, and a theological and philosophical framework built on a biblical worldview. All of this is carefully and thoughtfully developed, so we should not dismiss theory. "Theory" gets at the *why* behind what we do, after all!

And what about practice? Our practices as teachers are all the actions, the "teacher moves" we use. There are a great many practices we use in our work as teachers, from designing a learning environment, to developing curriculum materials, to preparing learning activities, to selecting instructional strategies, to devising assessments, to communicating learning. Now, ideally, these practices will flow out of the theories (we say) we believe. That is, our practices should be the way we live out what we believe in theory.

But here's the trouble: as I've already admitted, I see so many places in my own teaching practice where theory and practice just don't line up very well. I say I believe things . . . but my actions don't seem to flow out of those beliefs. And then it's a fair question to wonder whether I *really* believe those things I say I believe! I suspect every self-reflective teacher who cares deeply about their teaching will be able to point out areas where this mismatch between theory and practice is evident in their work as well.

Perhaps acknowledging this gap between theory and practice makes "teaching Christianly" feel a little hollow? Maybe you're thinking, "I say I believe a lot of things . . . but what if my actions don't really link to these beliefs?" If so, you are in good company! Many Christian teachers grapple with this very issue.

Let me encourage you to take this approach: what if we embody teaching Christianly by striving to shrink the gap between theory and practice? Perhaps teaching Christianly means seeking to continually evaluate not just what we are doing, but also *why we are doing it* . . . and striving to align our beliefs and our practices more and more closely.

I find I need to be regularly nudged towards this kind of closer alignment. One silly-but-helpful way of nudging myself along was a little sign I had taped to my desk for several years. It looked like this:[110]

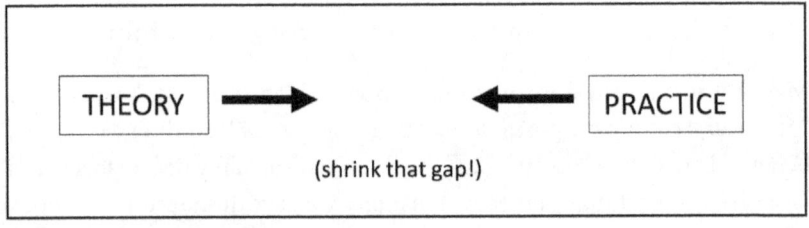

I kept this sign right in front of me, in a space where I regularly sat while doing the work of devising unit plans, grading students' papers, writing emails to parents, and developing curriculum materials. Every time I saw it, I felt a positive prodding to keep working at aligning what I do to what I *really* believe, and to not "simply teach." It's demanding work to continually do this! But it also becomes more of a habit over time, the more you work at it. And the truth I've discovered is this: some of the most joyful parts work as an educator have been the process of shrinking the gap, which I now see as the key to teaching Christianly. This is my encouragement to you, teacher: keep revising, keep refining, keep reimagining. Keep on working at shrinking that gap between theory and practice!

Imagining What is Next

We never "arrive" at teaching Christianly. Our journey to more fully living out our faith as Christians who teach is a life-long endeavor! This chapter includes many ideas about what teaching Christianly looks like, and I hope you are expanding your imagination of not just what teaching Christianly is, but also how to work at it. Because it *does* take work! But it is good work. It is joyful work!

I want to give you three specific words of encouragement on your journey towards teaching Christianly that I hope will guide you along the path and give you a burst of inspiration to keep moving forward, following Jesus. I hope these will enliven your imagination for what comes next for you in your development as a faithful Christian teacher.

First, remember that Jesus is Lord. Your actions throughout your teaching practice should be a proclamation saying, "Jesus is Lord in my classroom!" We often talk about teaching as a profession, meaning that we should be ethical and conscientious in our actions—and we obviously should aim for this kind of professionalism. But in all seriousness, teaching Christianly is a whole different kind of profession: the aim of teaching Christianly is a profession (a declaration) of your faith in Christ! The encouragement here is that this is not an obligation, something that we "have to" do. Living out a "Jesus is Lord" life in your work as a teacher is something we *get* to do! Never forget that teaching Christianly is a calling, a way to live out our broader calling to follow Jesus through our work in the classroom. And truly, this is a "We *get* to do this!" sort of opportunity to serve in his kingdom!

Second, realize that the call to teach Christianly is a call to love. Early in this book we discussed the three loves all teachers must have: to love *who* we teach, *what* we teach, and *how* to teach. And then we added a fourth love for Christian teachers to consider: a love of continually examining the impact of our faith on our teaching. Love is central to Christian faith. The Apostle John teaches us that God *is* love[111], and that "since God so loved us, we also ought to love one another."[112] This echoes Jesus's own teaching; when he was asked about the most important commandment, Jesus replied: "Love the Lord your God with all your heart and with all your soul and with all your mind and with all your strength.' The second is this: 'Love your neighbor as yourself.' There is no commandment greater than these."[113] These are key reminders for us as we imagine teaching Christianly: all our work should point towards our love of the Lord. And how do we embody this love of the Lord? We love our neighbors as we love ourselves—our students, their parents, our colleagues, administrators, community members, and rippling out into the world, we live our faith by loving the people God places in our path.

Finally, recognize that you are a work in progress. Christ's redeeming work is done, thanks be to God! But you and I are continually being made more and more into the likeness of Christ.[114] But God is not finished with us yet, and as we continue to grow in holiness, there will certainly still be times where we fall short. Don't let this stop you from striving to follow Jesus more faithfully! I love the story of Mother Teresa as an example of this. Mother Teresa was a Roman Catholic nun who served the poorest of the poor people in Kolkata, India for decades. She and the nuns who worked alongside her provided dignified care for people who were sick and dying. She was once asked by a reporter if she felt her ministry had been successful, since there are always more poor people for her to care for. Her response, I think, is insightful for us: "We are not called to be successful, but to be faithful."[115] This is a good word for us, as we strive to teach Christianly. Of course, we will want to be successful—that is natural and normal for us as human beings! But our calling is not success; our calling is to faithfully follow Jesus.

Teacher, you have the blessing and opportunity to do this good work. Remember that Jesus is Lord, and that we *get* to serve in his kingdom. Realize that you are called to love God and to love your neighbors, which is a tangible demonstration of your love for God. Recognize that you are a work in progress, and that you are called to be faithful, not successful. May these ideas capture your imagination for how you live out your faith by teaching Christianly! Grace and peace to you as you continue the journey of "always becoming" as you faithfully follow Jesus.

Questions for Reflection after Reading

1. As you consider the list of different views presented in this chapter of what teaching Christianly looks like in practice, which one(s) most resonate with you? Why?
2. What is a new idea that helped expand your imagination?
3. What challenged your thinking, or what question would you like answered?

Notes

Chapter 1: Learning to Think Like a Teacher: Developing Your "Teacher Imagination"

1. Palmer, *Courage to Teach*, 5.
2. Describing the premise of the book, Palmer says, "good teaching cannot be reduced to technique; good teaching comes from the identity and integrity of the teacher" (*Courage to Teach*, 10).
3. See chapter 7 in Palmer, *Courage to Teach*, which is entitled "Divided No More: Teaching from a Heart of Hope" for a careful treatment of this topic.
4. This idea was formulated by James K. A. Smith, in his excellent book *Desiring the Kingdom*, which includes this gem: "What if education . . . is not primarily about the absorption of ideas and information, but about the formation of hearts and desires? What if we began by appreciating how education not only gets into our head but also (and fundamentally) grabs us by the gut—what the New Testament refers to as *kardia*, 'the heart'? What if education was primarily concerned with shaping our hopes and passions—our visions of 'the good life'—and not merely about the dissemination of data and information as inputs to our thinking? What if the primary work of education was the transforming of our imagination rather than the saturation of our intellect? And what if this had as much to do with our bodies as with our minds?" (Smith, *Desiring the Kingdom*, 17–18).

Chapter 2: The Teaching Profession: Job? Calling? What Are We Doing Here Anyway?

5. Jer 1:5, *New International Version*.
6. Jer 1:6, *New International Version*.
7. Jer 1:7–10, *New International Version*.
8. Matt 16:24, *New International Version*.
9. This quote is the whole of the brief preface to Garber's excellent book, *Visions of Vocation: Common Grace for the Common Good*.

10. Garber, *Visions of Vocation*, 56.

11. Buechner, *Wishful Thinking*, 119. This lovely line comes at the end of a section in which Buechner discusses what calling—vocation—is really all about. Here is the larger section that this quote concludes: "There are all different kinds of voices calling you to all different kinds of work, and the problem is to find out which is the voice of God rather than of Society, say, or the Super-ego, or Self-Interest. By and large a good rule for finding out is this. The kind of work God usually calls you to is the kind of work (*a*) that you need most to do and (*b*) that the world most needs to have done. If you really get a kick out of your work, you've presumably met requirement (*a*), but if your work is writing TV deodorant commercials, the chances are you've missed requirement (*b*). On the other hand, if your work is being a doctor in a leper colony, you have probably met requirement (*b*), but if most of the time you're bored and depressed by it, the chances are you have not only bypassed (*a*) but probably aren't helping your patients much either. Neither the hair shirt nor the soft berth will do. The place God calls you to is the place where your deep gladness and the world's deep hunger meet" (Beuchner, *Wishful Thinking*, 118–19).

Chapter 3: Faith Matters: What Is Teaching "Christianly?"

12. I particularly appreciate James K. A. Smith's book *You Are What You Love: The Spiritual Power of Habit* for shaping my thinking about the religious nature of every human being.

13. Smith encourages us to think of our worldview as fundamentally being what we *love*, rather than what we *think*. We might say we believe certain things, but our actions might belie our *actual* beliefs. Thinking about this in terms of what we love can help us reimagine how our daily habits and practices shape our beliefs, and how what we *really* believe will in turn influence what we do as we move through the world.

14. In his book, *Cause of Christian Education*, Edlin unpacks the idea of "everyone is religious" carefully and in great detail in his first chapter, which is entitled "No Neutrality and Why It Matters." In this chapter, he argues that an effort to exclude Christian faith from the classroom is in fact another religious perspective being embodied. Edlin says, "Another area of pedagogy that demonstrates no neutrality is the selection of resources for the classroom. It is not possible to teach everything, or to expose students to every possible resource. Accordingly, textbook publishers and teachers carefully select the resources for teaching, and the in- formation that will be taught. These selections are made based upon what the selectors *believe* to be the most important resources and experiences. There it is again: we cannot escape the reality that beliefs are central in shaping students' learning experience. There is no neutrality" (Edlin, *Cause of Christian Education*, 9.) This is a specific example about choosing which resources should be included or excluded in the classroom, but this general approach is what I'm getting at when I suggest that everyone is religious—everyone has some sort of operating belief structure that guides not just how they teach, but how they *are* in the world.

15. I am deeply indebted to John Van Dyk, and his impressive body of work related to the concept of teaching Christianly. His extensive writing about teaching Christianly has thoroughly impacted the way I think about, talk about, and practice teaching Christianly. In particular, his books *Letters to Lisa: Conversations with a Christian Teacher* and *The Craft of Christian Teaching: A Classroom Journey* have been incredibly important to my development as a Christian educator. My copy of *The Craft of Christian Teaching* is literally falling apart because it has been read so many times! I should really just buy a new copy, but the one I have on my shelf today has all my underlining and margin notes, and it documents my own journey to learning more and more how to take my faith seriously and let Jesus guide my classroom practice.

16. Luke 9:23, *New International Version*.

Chapter 4: Joys and Challenges of Teaching Today: History, Reform, and Looking to the Future

17. I must be clear here that I am writing about American education specifically because that is the cultural context I know firsthand from having spent my whole professional career teaching in American educational institutions. I am less familiar with the educational history of other countries. The brief history in this chapter is meant to illustrate my point that shifts in school culture mirrors broader cultural shifts. I do not mean to suggest that the story of American educational history is the example everyone should aspire towards. Also, there are whole books devoted to the history of American education that get into much greater depth and detail than the brief sketch I'm laying out here. The point is to illustrate some of the historical shifts that have led to the present era of American education.

18. National Commission on Educational Excellence, *Nation at Risk*, 5. You can read this report for yourself in its entirety online; a quick online search will allow you to find a full copy. It's a fascinating snapshot of what educational reformers in the early 1980s were thinking.

19. Eccl 1:9–11, *New International Version*.

20. Van Dyk, *Letters to Lisa*, 6.

21. The Rev. Dr. Verlyn Boone used to use this encouragement at the end of many of his sermons when he pastored our church. Learning this truth has shaped my own view of God and my relationship to him immeasurably!

22. Van Dyk, *Letters to Lisa*, 9.

Chapter 5: Do the Right Thing: Professionalism and Ethics

23. Genesis 1:27 says, "So God created mankind in his own image, in the image of God he created them; male and female he created them."

24. Fredrick Buechner shares this lovely thought on creativity: "To *make* suggests

making something out of something else the way a carpenter makes wooden boxes out of wood. To *create* suggest making something out of nothing the way an artist makes paintings or poems. It is true that artists, like carpenters, have to use something else—paint, words—but the beauty or meaning they make is different from the materials they make it out of. To create is to make something essentially new." (*Wishful Thinking*, 20).

25. The National Education Association is the largest teacher's union in the United States with millions of members. Their Code of Ethics for Educators can be accessed on their website: https://www.nea.org/resource-library/code-ethics-educators.

26. Van Dyk, *Craft of Christian Teaching*, 197.

Chapter 6: Understanding Your Office: Learning and Leading

27. David Smith has a helpful exploration of "power spots" in the classroom. Smith recounts a story of a teacher temporarily in charge of a colleague's classroom who happened to stand in the "power spot" in the classroom, which dramatically impacted the way the students in that class responded to him. (See *On Christian Teaching*, 117–18.) This an important reminder for teachers; students have some expectations of the way that teachers wield power in the classroom, and have been conditioned to respond in particular ways when teachers are engaging students from power spots.

28 Van Dyk reminds us, "As a Christian teacher you need to develop a sense of *office consciousness*. Such office consciousness guarantees that you will not reduce teaching to a humdrum menial task, a routine for which you receive a monthly paycheck. Office consciousness will help you to connect your work to the calling of God, and therefore, to the work of God himself. Office consciousness equips you to see that every morning anew you enter the classroom as a place where the Kingdom of God must come to expression. Office consciousness reminds you that together with others you must strive to do his will" (*Craft of Christian Teaching*, 41).

29. Van Dyk addresses this idea of legitimate authority as well, saying, "Authority is inseparably attached to office. This reality is true for all forms of office. My authority as a father, for example, is to be attributed to my *office* as father rather than too my size, age, or accumulated wisdom. If we disconnect authority from office and attach it to ourselves as persons, we change legitimate authority into raw power" (Van Dyk, *Craft of Christian Teaching*, 46).

30. Here I am drawing on Daniel Pink's work in *Drive: The Surprising Truth about What Motivates Us*. Pink uses the concept of an asymptote to illustrate mastery—something which we can never quite achieve, and yet we keep chasing. This profoundly captures my sense of what the teaching profession looks like: mastery of our practice is something we continue to strive towards, but will never achieve on this side of glory.

31. Van Dyk has a lovely bit about this idea at the end *Letters to Lisa*. Reflecting on the challenges of teaching Christianly, Van Dyk writes, "The term may be nothing but jargon to some, but, to be honest, I've actually found the concept of office consciousness helpful—especially when I'm down and blue and wonder whether I

Notes

really should have become a teacher. You know of such times, too, when it looks as if the job is just too overwhelming. Whenever that happens—sometimes too often!—I do two things: First, I pray. Then I remember that God has called me to the office of teacher... the Lord does not call us to a task we can't do. He equips us" (*Letters to Lisa*, 190).

Chapter 7: Jesus Loves the Little Children: Learner Development

32. Luke 18:16–17, *New International Version*.
33. See Matt 18:1–9 for this story in context.
34. Gen 1:27, *New International Version*.
35. Gen 1:31, *New International Version*.
36. Wolters puts it this way: "We must stress that the Bible teaches plainly that Adam and Eve's fall into sin was not just an isolated act of disobedience, but an event of catastrophic significance for creation as a whole. Not only the whole human race but the whole nonhuman world too was caught up in the train of Adam's failure to heed God's explicit commandment and warning. The effects of sin touch all of creation; no created thing is in principle untouched by the corrosive effects of the fall" (*Creation Regained*, 53).
37. Lord's Day 3 of the Heidelberg Catechism uses this language to describe human sinfulness. Q&A 7 says it this way: "The fall and disobedience of our first parents, Adam and Eve, in Paradise. This fall has so poisoned our nature that we are all conceived and born in a sinful condition."
38. Rom 3:11, *New International Version*.
39. Wolters explores the relationship between the goodness of creation and the corrosive effects of the fall this way: "The central point to make is that, biblically speaking, sin neither abolishes nor becomes identified with creation. Creation and sin remain distinct, however closely they may be intertwined in our experience... evil does not have the power of brining too naught God's steadfast faithfulness to the works of his hands" (*Creation Regained*, 57).
40. Wolters puts it this way: "Through Christ, God determined 'to reconcile to himself *all things*,' [emphasis in original] writes Paul (Col 1:20)... The scope of redemption is as great as the fall; it embraces creation as a whole" (*Creation Regained*, 72).
41. See Wolters, *Creation Regained*, 83–86.
42. Rom 3:23–24, *New International Version*.
43. Syd Hielema is a blessing to the church! He served as a Professor of Theology at both Dordt University and Redeemer University College, and then as the Director of the Faith Formation Ministries of the Christian Reformed Church in North America.
44. James Fowler's Stages of Faith is one popular model used by many Christians interested in spiritual development. Fowler unpacks his research in his book, *Stages of Faith: The Psychology of Human Development and the Quest for Meaning*.

45. One such tool is called FaithJourney—a web-based portfolio system being used by some Christian schools and churches to document and nurture faith formation and discipleship. You can learn more about this tool and how it works at https://myfaithjourney.com/.

46. Mark 12:29–31, *New International Version*.

47. Andy Crouch's marvelous book, *The Life We're Looking For: Reclaiming Relationship in a Technological World* is one of the best books I've read in recent years. It is challenging, thought-provoking, and encouraging for people seeking to faithfully follow Jesus in a high-tech world. This quote comes from page 33, where he is in the midst of unpacking a biblical view of what it means to be human.

48. Crouch, *Life We're Looking For*, 33. This is definition serves as the foundation for the rest of the entire book.

49. Smith, *You Are What You Love*, 3. In the book, Smith argues that Christians often over-emphasize faith as a purely cognitive exercise, rather than recognizing the essential role our hearts, souls, and even bodies play in worship.

50. See 1 John 4:7–21. "God is love" is directly from verse 16. And "We love because he first loved us," is 1 John 4:19. We are called to a life of loving our neighbors!

Chapter 8: Jesus Loves ALL the Little Children: Learner Diversity

51. Rev 7:9–10, *New International Version*.

52. A quick search through an academic database will result in hundreds of peer-reviewed papers that illustrate this finding. One example that is readable and succinct—and a bit depressing: "The achievement gap fails to close" by Hanushek et al.

53. Canada, for example, has two official languages: English and French. South Africa has eleven. Bolivia has thirty-seven official languages! The United States of America has no official language, but English is the language most often used in schools—and often assumed to be "official."

54. Perhaps you have taken an IQ test before? IQ stands for "intelligence quotient," and there are various IQ tests available. The Stanford-Binet test is very popular, as is the Wechsler test, which includes a separate section on verbal intelligence.

Chapter 9: Culture and Climate: Creating a Space Where Learning Can Happen

55. Van Dyk encourages us to "check your classroom atmosphere. Is your classroom a pleasant, happy place in which students are encouraged to help each other and work together? Or does it resemble a zoo full of wild animals eager to devour one another.? Do the children trust you and each other, and do you trust them? Or is your classroom atmosphere choking with fear and suspicion?" (*Letters to Lisa*, 7.) As he continues in this section, Van Dyk admonishes Christian educators to carefully

consider the role we play in the classroom through modeling Christlike behavior, giving encouragement to students, providing for a safe classroom environment, and disciplining students in a way that focuses on restoration and relationship. A tall order, for sure!

56. Ginott, *Teacher and Child*, 15–16.

57. 1 Cor 12:21, *New International Version*.

58. Buechner says, "Happiness turns up more or less where you'd expect it to—a good marriage, a rewarding job, a pleasant vacation. Joy, on the other hand, is as notoriously unpredictable as the one who bequeaths it" (*Wishful Thinking*, 58). This is a good reminder for us, I think, that joy may be something we *pursue*, and stumble onto as we seek to follow the way of Jesus.

59. Van Dyk, *Craft of Christian Teaching*, 77. The whole section from pp. 77–82 is a helpful introduction into the idea of what the craft of Christian teaching looks like in practice.

60. Smith, *On Christian Teaching*, 12.

Chapter 10: Knowledge and Understanding: What Do You Need to Know to Be a Teacher?

61. The idea of pedagogical content knowledge was proposed by Lee Shulman in his 1985 address to the American Educational Research Association. He wrote and published several articles throughout the 1980s and 1990s on this topic, and many other educational researchers have found this model to be very useful for thinking about the interaction of pedagogy and content knowledge. Much ongoing research in education right up to today draws upon Shulman's work.

62 Shulman, "Those Who Understand," 9.

63. Ps 19:1–2, *New International Version*.

64. Prov 25:1, *New International Version*.

65. I Kings 4:29–34 says, "God gave Solomon wisdom and very great insight, and a breadth of understanding as measureless as the sand on the seashore. Solomon's wisdom was greater than the wisdom of all the people of the East, and greater than all the wisdom of Egypt. He was wiser than anyone else, including Ethan the Ezrahite—wiser than Heman, Kalkol and Darda, the sons of Mahol. And his fame spread to all the surrounding nations. He spoke three thousand proverbs and his songs numbered a thousand and five. He spoke about plant life, from the cedar of Lebanon to the hyssop that grows out of walls. He also spoke about animals and birds, reptiles and fish. From all nations people came to listen to Solomon's wisdom, sent by all the kings of the world, who had heard of his wisdom."

66. You really should read Job 38–41 for yourself! It is an incredible picture of God's power and might on display. God's response to Job illustrates that God does not owe human beings any explanation. And yet, he reveals himself to us through creation, and his love and care for us—and Job—comes through as well.

67. Job 42:2–6, *New International Version*.

68. Prov 1:7, *New International Version*.

Chapter 11: Finding the Path: Curriculum Guides the Learning

69. The metaphor of the teacher as a guide is one I borrowed from Van Dyk. He writes about this quite extensively in *Craft of Christian Teaching*. See chapters 7 and 8 of that book for an elaboration of Van Dyk's approach.

70. In *Textbook and the Lecture*, Friesen lays out a history of media in education, including the development of textbooks. Modern textbooks the way we might picture them today were developed in the 1600s and 1700s. Friesen argues that Martin Luther's Lesser Catechism, published in 1529, is one of the key predecessors to contemporary textbooks, including questions and summaries of scripture that a priest or pastor could draw from to help instruct catechumens in the doctrines of the church. See chapter 7, "A Textbook Case" for the detailed history and development of textbooks.

71. I'm drawing on Van Dyk here again, in particular *Craft of Christian Teaching*, 99–104.

72. Heb 12:1b–2a, *New International Version*.

Chapter 12: Designs for Learning: Planning and Preparation for Effective Instruction

73. Wiggins and McTighe introduce these two problematic approaches as the "twin sins of design" in the introduction to their excellent book *Understanding by Design*.

74. Wiggins and McTighe, *Understanding by Design*, 3.

75. Van Brummelen, *Walking with God in the Classroom*, 132.

76. Van Dyk gets at this when he says, "Particularly demanding is the difficult task of keeping your students involved in their learning in a sustained way. Planning interesting, effective lessons on a daily basis is just plain hard, even exhausting, and sometimes discouraging work for both beginning teachers and seasoned veterans" (*Craft of Christian Teaching*, 4). This captures it well!

77. David Smith includes an excellent example of what this sort of focus on learning looks like in chapter 2 of his book, *On Christian Teaching: Practicing Faith in the Classroom*. He describes how he intentionally reimagined the first 9 minutes of the first class meeting of the semester in his German class to better invite students into his classroom, assess their current level of understanding, build community, and give them a sense of the kind of work they will do in the course. All of this is aimed at meeting his intended learning outcomes for the course, engaging his students more fully in the learning, and living out his faith in his classroom more authentically.

78. This quote is widely attributed to Linus Pauling; the best source I've found for it was

that Francis Crick (one of the discoverers of the structure of DNA who worked with Pauling earlier in his career) quoted Pauling as having said this. Crick's quotation was in a speech he gave at a symposium on the impact of Pauling's work at Oregon State University in 1995, the year after Pauling's death. Pauling is right, in my experience: we might have many terrible ideas, but having lots of ideas, and being willing to pursue them at least a little way down the road is perhaps the best way to find really great ideas!

79. Smith, *On Christian Teaching*, 71.

Chapter 13: Getting Inside their Heads: The Most Mystical Part of Teaching

80. It is a great idea to involve your students your decision-making process about what kinds of work you'll assign, and how you'll evaluate their learning. Van Dyk's advice about how involving students in these decisions can bolster a positive classroom environment is instructive: "Evaluation procedures, too, should, involve the students. Ask for student input on constructing rubrics, on designing portfolios, on what constitutes passing and failure or fair evaluation procedures. Invite them to frame review, test, and evaluation instruments. These activities contribute to a good collaborative environment" (*Craft of Christian Teaching*, 136).

81. I like Harro Van Brummelen's take on the difference between assessment and evaluation. He uses the example of a kindergarten teacher checking on students' knowledge of the letters of the alphabet: "A kindergarten teacher may determine that a student recognizes twenty of the twenty-six capital letters in the alphabet (assessment). Near the start of kindergarten she may interpret that as very good progress, but at the end of the year she may consider the same thing to be a cause for concern (evaluation)" (*Walking with God in the Classroom*, 139.) I think this helps us to picture what kinds of professional judgments all teachers make when evaluating their students' progress.

82. A rubric is an evaluation tool that illustrates different categories to be evaluated and gives descriptions for different levels of performance for each of those categories. Rubrics can give students and teachers alike more clarity into what constitutes exemplary work.

83. Wormeli, *Fair Isn't Always Equal: Assessing and Grading in the Differentiated Classroom*, 200. Wormeli's book is full of wisdom for teachers in thinking through their assessment and evaluation procedures, and I highly recommend it to all teachers interested in improving their practices.

84. This idea was further cemented for me after reading Elaine Brouwer's powerful article, "Assessment for Learning: A Blessing for our Students." In this piece, Brower thoughtfully articulates the ways that our formative assessment practices can hurt or heal, can punish or bless. It will almost certainly challenge you, but I suspect it will also encourage you.

85. Matt 7:1a, *New International Version*.

86. Matt 7:1–5, *New International Version*.

Chapter 14: Effective Instruction: Teaching like Jesus?

87. Take Paul's teaching, for example, in Eph 1:18–21: "I pray that the eyes of your heart may be enlightened in order that you may know the hope to which he has called you, the riches of his glorious inheritance in his holy people, and his incomparably great power for us who believe. That power is the same as the mighty strength he exerted when he raised Christ from the dead and seated him at his right hand in the heavenly realms, far above all rule and authority, power and dominion, and every name that is invoked, not only in the present age but also in the one to come."

88. See, for example, John 1:1–3: "In the beginning was the Word, and the Word was with God, and the Word was God. He was with God in the beginning. Through him all things were made; without him nothing was made that has been made."

89. See, for example, 2 Cor 5:17–19: "Therefore, if anyone is in Christ, the new creation has come: The old has gone, the new is here! All this is from God, who reconciled us to himself through Christ and gave us the ministry of reconciliation: that God was reconciling the world to himself in Christ, not counting people's sins against them. And he has committed to us the message of reconciliation."

90. See Jesus's words in Rev 22:12–13: "Look, I am coming soon! My reward is with me, and I will give to each person according to what they have done. I am the Alpha and the Omega, the First and the Last, the Beginning and the End."

91. See Jesus's interaction with Peter in Matt 16:15–17: "'But what about you?' [Jesus] asked. 'Who do you say I am?' Simon Peter answered, 'You are the Messiah, the Son of the living God.' Jesus replied, 'Blessed are you, Simon son of Jonah, for this was not revealed to you by flesh and blood, but by my Father in heaven.'" Peter got it!

92. John 12:16, *New International Version*.

93. I highly recommend Rick Wormeli's book, *Fair Isn't Always Equal* for a host of strategies for teaching and assessing diverse groups of students.

94. Educational research into effective teaching methods has been going on for decades. Two widely cited books that synthesize some of this research are John Hattie's *Visible Learning* and Marzano, Pickering, and Pollock's *Classroom Instruction that Work*. Updated editions of *Classroom Instruction that Works* that incorporate new research were released in 2012 and 2022.

95. The reality of teachers teaching the way they were taught is not surprising, and it appears throughout the research literature in the field of education reaching back to the 1970s. In his 1975 book *Schoolteacher: A Sociological Perspective*, Lortie described this phenomenon as "the apprenticeship of observation" (160). Again, to be clear, the problem is not that teaching as we were taught means we will be ineffective, but that there may be much *more* effective strategies for ensuring students will learn.

96. See Van Dyk, *Craft of Christian Teaching*, 162 for a thoughtful articulation of some of the strengths of direct instruction.

Notes

97. Van Dyk says, "Get the kids involved! All good teachers know that the more the students are involved in their learning, the better they will learn" (*Craft of Christian Teaching*, 165). In my experience, this is true! But that doesn't mean it's easy... this approach still takes plenty of planning and development for it to be effective.

98. I first encountered the idea of the 60 Percent Strategy in a graduate course I once took with Van Dyk. This is not a research-based strategy; it is a gut feeling I have as an experienced educator who has done a fair bit of experimenting and exploration with a wide variety of direct and indirect teaching strategies at a variety of grade levels and in different content areas.

Chapter 15: Joy on the Journey: Why We Never "Arrive" at Teaching Christianly

99. Van Dyk, *Craft of Christian Teaching*, 33.

100. Van Dyk spends a whole chapter in *Craft of Christian Teaching* unpacking different views on what teaching Christianly means, and how different Christian teachers might approach this work. In this section I draw heavily on the themes he brings up in that chapter. See Van Dyk, *Craft of Christian Teaching*, 19–28.

101. I do not have space here to devote to fully fleshing out this idea, but I would recommend to you Wolter's excellent book, *Creation Regained* which is useful for understanding the contours of a Reformational worldview, but in chapter 4 he unpacks this idea of Christ's sovereignty in great detail.

102. See Gal 5:22–23, where the apostle Paul teaches, "But the fruit of the Spirit is love, joy, peace, forbearance, kindness, goodness, faithfulness, gentleness, and self-control. Against such things there is no law."

103. Jas 2:14, *New International Version*.

104. See Luke 10: 25–37

105. Mark 10:30, *New International Version*.

106. Matt 28:19–20, *New International Version*.

107. See Matt 5–7.

108. In all seriousness, you should pause and read the first few chapters of the book of Acts. The apostles are transformed by the indwelling of the Holy Spirit in ways that seem almost incredible given the way they bumbled around following Jesus in the gospels. Their preparation for their calling as apostles was certainly in their formation, but the Spirit empowered them to live it out!

109. Jas 3:1, *New International Version*.

110. This was an idea I got from Van Dyk in a course I took with him as a graduate student. A small reminder to keep an awareness of my ongoing development in teaching Christianly!

111. 1 John 4:16 says, "And so we know and rely on the love God has for us. God is love. Whoever lives in love lives in God, and God in them."

112. 1 John 4:11, *New International Version*.

113. Mark 12:30–31, *New International Version*.

114. See Rom 8:28–30, for example: "And we know that in all things God works for the good of those who love him, who[i] have been called according to his purpose. For those God foreknew he also predestined to be conformed to the image of his Son, that he might be the firstborn among many brothers and sisters. And those he predestined, he also called; those he called, he also justified; those he justified, he also glorified.")

115. Sala, *40 Unstoppable Women who Changed the World*, 61.

Bibliography

Brouwer, Elaine. "Assessment for Learning: A Blessing for our Students." *Christian Educators Journal* 47 (2007) 6–9.
Buechner, Frederick. *Wishful Thinking: A Seeker's ABC*. San Francisco: Harper, 1993.
Crouch, Andy. *The Life We're Looking For: Reclaiming Relationship in a Technological World*. New York: Convergent, 2022.
Edlin, Richard J. *The Cause of Christian Education*. 4th ed. Sioux Center, IA: Dordt, 2014.
Fowler, James W. *Stages of Faith: The Psychology of Human Development and the Quest for Meaning*. San Francisco: Harper & Row, 1981.
Friesen, Norm. *The Textbook and the Lecture: Education in the Age of New Media*. Baltimore: Johns Hopkins University Press, 2017.
Garber, Steven. *Visions of Vocation: Common Grace for the Common Good*. Downers Grove, IL: InterVarsity, 2014.
Ginott, Haim. *Teacher and Child*. New York: Macmillan, 1972.
Hanushek, Eric A., et al. "The achievement gap fails to close." *Education Next* 19 (2019) 8–17.
Hattie, John. *Visible Learning: A Synthesis of Over 800 Meta-Analyses Relating to Achievement*. Abingdon, UK: Routledge, 2008.
Lortie, Dan C. *Schoolteacher: A Sociological Perspective*. Chicago: University of Chicago Press, 1975.
Marzano, Robert J., et al. *Classroom Instruction that Works: Research-Based Strategies for Increasing Student Achievement*. Alexandria, VA: ASCD, 2001.
National Commission on Excellence in Education. *A Nation at Risk: The Imperative for Educational Reform*. Washington, DC: National Commission on Excellence in Education, 1983. https://edreform.com/wp-content/uploads/2013/02/A_Nation_At_Risk_1983.pdf.
National Educators Association. *Code of Ethics for Educators*. Washington, DC: National Educators Association, 1975. https://www.nea.org/resource-library/code-ethics-educators
Palmer, Parker J. *The Courage to Teach: Exploring the Inner Landscape of a Teacher's Life*. San Francisco: Jossey-Bass, 1998.
Pink, Daniel H. *Drive: The Surprising Truth about What Motivates Us*. New York: Penguin, 2011.
Sala, Harold. *40 Unstoppable Women who Changed the World*. Peabody, MA: Aspire, 2021
Shulman, Lee S. "Those Who Understand: Knowledge Growth in Teaching." *Educational Researcher* 15 (1986) 4–14.

Bibliography

Smith, David I. *On Christian Teaching: Practicing Faith in the Classroom.* Grand Rapids: Eerdmans, 2018.

Smith, James K. A. *Desiring the Kingdom: Worship, Worldview, and Cultural Formation.* Grand Rapids: Baker Academic, 2009.

———. *You Are What You Love: The Spiritual Power of Habit* Grand Rapids: Brazos, 2016.

Ursinus, Zacharias, and Olevianus, Caspar. *Heidelberg Catechism.* Heidelberg, Germany: 1563. https://www.crcna.org/welcome/beliefs/confessions/heidelberg-catechism.

Van Brummelen, Harro. *Walking with God in the Classroom: Christian Approaches to Teaching and Learning.* 3rd ed. Colorado Springs, CO: Purposeful Design, 2009.

Van Dyk, J. *The Craft of Christian Teaching: A Classroom Journey.* Sioux Center, IA: Dordt, 2000.

———. *Letters to Lisa: Conversations with a Christian Teacher.* Sioux Center, IA: Dordt, 1997.

Wiggins, Grant P., and Jay McTighe. *Understanding by Design.* 2nd ed. Alexandria, VA: ACSD, 2005.

Wolters, Albert M. *Creation Regained: Biblical Basics for a Reformational Worldview.* Grand Rapids: Eerdmans, 2005.

Wormeli, Rick. *Fair Isn't Always Equal: Assessing and Grading in the Differentiated Classroom.* Portland, ME: Stenhouse, 2006.

www.ingramcontent.com/pod-product-compliance
Lightning Source LLC
Chambersburg PA
CBHW020850160426
43192CB00007B/869